50 Unforgettable Motorcycle Journeys
on the Island of Newfoundland

ROAMING THE ROCK

Harry O'Reilly

BOULDER
BOOKS

Library and Archives Canada Cataloguing in Publication

Title: Roaming the Rock : 50 unforgettable motorcycle journeys
on the island of Newfoundland / Harry O'Reilly.
Names: O'Reilly, Harry, author.
Description: Includes index.
Identifiers: Canadiana 20240305523 | ISBN 9781989417898 (softcover)
Subjects: LCSH: Motorcycle touring—Newfoundland and Labrador—Guidebooks.
| LCSH: Newfoundland and
    Labrador—Description and travel. | LCSH: Newfoundland
and Labrador—Guidebooks. | LCGFT:
    Guidebooks.
Classification: LCC GV1059.53.C3 O74 2024 | DDC 917.1804/5—dc23

Published by Boulder Books
Portugal Cove-St. Philip's, Newfoundland and Labrador
www.boulderbooks.ca

Interior design and layout: Tanya Montini
Cover design: Tanya Montini
Editor: Stephanie Porter
Copy editor: Iona Bulgin

Printed in China

We acknowledge the financial support of the Government of Newfoundland and Labrador
through the Department of Tourism, Culture, Arts and Recreation.

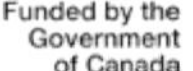

ROAMING THE ROCK

Table of Contents

Introduction
What Is the Rock? 10
How to Use This Guide 13

50 Bike Trips

Western Newfoundland
1   Southwestern Newfoundland, Route 470
    (*Channel-Port aux Basques to
    Rose Blanche-Harbour Le Cou*) 17
2   Codroy Valley (*Channel-Port aux Basques
    to Cape Anguille*) 23
3   Bay St. George South (*Crabbes River Park
    to Highlands to Journois*) 29
4   Port au Port Peninsula 33
5   Burgeo plus Ferries 39
6   Bay of Islands South 45
7   Bay of Islands North 49

Rose Blanche Lighthouse.

8 Deer Lake to Trout River *(TCH to Gros Morne National Park)* 53

9 Gros Morne National Park *(Wiltondale to Cow Head)* 59

10 Great Northern Peninsula North of Gros Morne National Park *(Three Mile Rock to Port au Choix)* 65

11 Gros Morne Coast *(Eddies Cove West to Plum Point)* 71

12 Labrador Coast *(Pidgeon Cove-St. Barbe, Newfoundland, to Red Bay, Labrador)* 77

13 Road to L'Anse aux Meadows National Historic Site *(Anchor Point to L'Anse aux Meadows)* 83

14 Top of Great Northern Peninsula *(St. Anthony Bight to Plum Point)* 89

15 Northeast Side of Great Northern Peninsula *(Main Brook to Englee)* 93

16 Southeast Side of Great Northern Peninsula *(Pasadena to Jackson's Arm)* 97

Central Newfoundland

17 Baie Verte Peninsula West 101

18 Baie Verte Peninsula East 107

19 Springdale Exit 111

20 South Brook Exit plus Ferries 115

21 Central Newfoundland *(Buchans to Bishop's Falls)* . . . 121

22 Botwood Exit 127

23 Connaigre Peninsula West plus Ferries 133

24 Connaigre Peninsula East plus Ferries 137

25 Bay of Exploits East *(Norris Arm to Laurenceton)* . . . 143

26 Lewisporte Loop 149

27 New World Island and Twillingate Islands 155

28 Change Islands 163

29 Fogo Island 167

30 Gander Loop 173

31 Eastport Peninsula plus Ferry 181

32 Terra Nova National Park and Environs *(Benton to Lethbridge)* 187

Port Saunders.

Eastern Newfoundland

33 Random Island and Surroundings
(*Clarenville to Winter Brook*) 193

34 Bonavista Peninsula, Discovery Trail
(*Southern Bay to Elliston*) 199

35 Bonavista Peninsula, Cabot Highway
(*Sweet Bay to Bonavista*) 203

36 Northern Burin Peninsula (*Goobies to Harbour Mille*). . . .209

37 Middle Burin Peninsula (*Marystown to
South East Bight plus Ferry*) 215

38 Southern Burin Peninsula
(*"Bottom of the Boot"*). 219

39 Isthmus of Avalon 225

40 Whitbourne to Cape St. Mary's 229

41 Dildo to Grates Cove 235

42 The Irish Loop 241

43 Conception Bay (*Harbour Grace to St. John's*) 247

44 Northeast Avalon (*Petty Harbour to Bell Island
to Petty Harbour*) 253

Boat Harbour.

Trans-Canada Highway

45 Channel-Port aux Basques to Stephenville 259

46 Stephenville to Howley 259

47 Howley to Badger. 259

48 Badger to Gambo 259

49 Gambo to Goobies 259

50 Goobies to St. John's 259

Index of place names 260

Note from the author 264

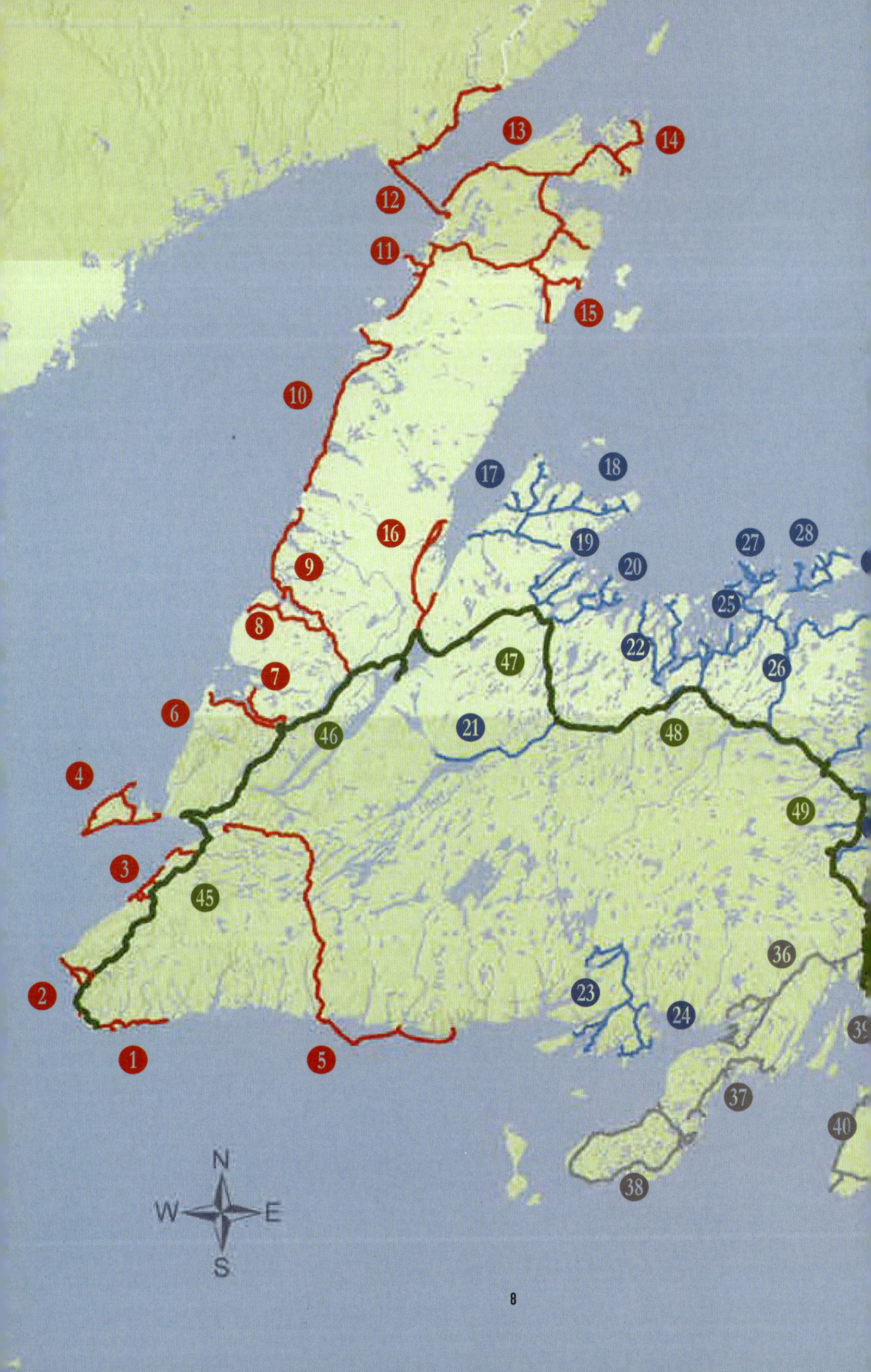

N
W E
S

Western Newfoundland

1   Southwestern Newfoundland
2   Codroy Valley
3   Bay St. George South
4   Port au Port Peninsula
5   Burgeo plus Ferries
6   Bay of Islands South
7   Bay of Islands North
8   Deer Lake to Trout River
9   Gros Morne National Park
10   Great Northern Peninsula North of Gros Morne National Park
11   Gros Morne Coast
12   Labrador Coast
13   Road to L'Anse aux Meadows National Historic Site
14   Top of Great Northern Peninsula
15   Northeast Side of Great Northern Peninsula
16   Southeast Side of Great Northern Peninsula

Central Newfoundland

17   Baie Verte Peninsula West
18   Baie Verte Peninsula East
19   Springdale Exit
20   South Brook Exit plus Ferries
21   Central Newfoundland
22   Botwood Exit
23   Connaigre Peninsula West plus Ferries
24   Connaigre Peninsula East plus Ferries
25   Bay of Exploits East
26   Lewisporte Loop
27   New World Island and Twillingate Islands
28   Change Islands
29   Fogo Island
30   Gander Loop
31   Eastport Peninsula plus Ferry
32   Terra Nova National Park and Environs

Eastern Newfoundland

33   Random Island and Surroundings
34   Bonavista Peninsula, Discovery Trail
35   Bonavista Peninsula, Cabot Highway
36   Northern Burin Peninsula
37   Middle Burin Peninsula
38   Southern Burin Peninsula
39   Isthmus of Avalon
40   Whitbourne to Cape St. Mary's
41   Dildo to Grates Cove
42   The Irish Loop
43   Conception Bay
44   Northeast Avalon

Trans-Canada Highway

45   Channel-Port aux Basques to Stephenville
46   Stephenville to Howley
47   Howley to Badger
48   Badger to Gambo
49   Gambo to Goobies
50   Goobies to St. John's

What Is the Rock?

Newfoundland and Labrador is the most easterly province in Canada—and *the Rock* refers to Newfoundland, the island part of the province.

Facts about the Rock
- It is the fourth largest island in Canada and 16th largest in the world.
- Its population is approximately 521,000 (as of 2023): 92 per cent on the island; 50 per cent of the island's population live on the Avalon Peninsula.
- Its area is approximately 111,390 square kilometres.
- It includes 7,000 other islands.
- Newfoundland Standard Time (NST) is 30 minutes ahead of the eastern North American continent—at 6 a.m. in Nova Scotia, it is already 6:30 a.m. on the Rock.

Motorcycling around the island of Newfoundland is the focus of this book, although I have included one day trip to Labrador.

Ferries to Newfoundland
Motorcyclists can reach Newfoundland by three ferries. Two cross from North Sydney, Nova Scotia, and are operated by Marine Atlantic; they arrive in Channel-Port aux Basques (5- to 7-hour crossing) or Argentia (16-hour crossing). The third leaves Blanc-Sablon, Quebec (adjacent to L'Anse-au-Clair, Labrador), and arrives in St. Barbe, Newfoundland (1.5-hour crossing).

Marine Atlantic ferries have ample room for cars, trucks, and motorcycles. If you book an overnight crossing, consider renting a cabin. I have travelled on these boats for at least 30 nights with my motorcycle and riding the following day is much easier after a night's sleep. Each cabin usually has several bunks, helpful for sharing costs when travelling with others. Book ahead of time at marineatlantic.ca.

Route 1, the Trans-Canada Highway (TCH), is a paved 900-kilometre thoroughfare across Newfoundland from Channel-Port aux Basques to St. John's. The Newfoundland section of the TCH is a two- to four-lane highway, and a full four-lane highway for the 90 kilometres heading into the capital, St. John's.

Bikers on a "Ride for Dad" fundraiser in Central Newfoundland.

Almost every route off the TCH suggested in this book is paved, with speed limits of 60 to 100 kilometres/hour. Any gravel roads are indicated as such.

Important information about riding in Newfoundland
- Windy conditions are frequent, particularly in coastal areas.
- Daytime travel is advisable; between dawn and dusk, moose, caribou, and bears are often spotted on or near the road.
- The best riding conditions are from May through September, although I ride from early April to early November.
- In early and late season, use electrically heated coat and gloves.
- Good tires and brakes are a necessity.
- Gas up often; there are sufficient gas stations around the island but you will encounter a few isolated stretches with no amenities, such as the 150-kilometre Burgeo Highway.
- Monitor the forecast but be aware that the weather is highly changeable; always carry rain gear.
- Restaurants and food trucks are plentiful, but carrying a snack is a good rule of thumb.

It's all about the journey and not the destination when motorcycling in Newfoundland. I always have back rests on my cruisers or touring bikes. Although the seats are usually comfortable on these big bikes, I like to get off every hour or so and enjoy the scenery, especially if I am alone with my camera.

Stay visible by wearing bright and colourful gear, from jacket to helmet. You will encounter some potholes as with any roads anywhere but, overall, Newfoundland's roads are well maintained.

How to Use This Guide

The 50 trips in this book include 11,000 kilometres of paved routes. Each trip is between 100 and 400 kilometres long and is a written as a return trip. The rides last 2 to 4 hours on any given day, or you may want to combine rides from the same region for a longer day trip. I always recommend building in time to get off your bike and take in the sights, visit museums, hike a trail, and chat with local residents.

Each trip writeup includes directions, as well highlights and history notes for each route. Population estimates are from 2016 and/or 2021 census information. At the top of each trip writeup is a box with brief notes about the trip: overall distance, primary roads travelled, and the location of amenities such as gas, restaurants, grocery stores, and accommodations. Each trip chapter includes a road map.

You will rarely be far from a gas station or other supply stop; particularly isolated stretches of road are identified as such. Businesses and related information mentioned in the text are current as of 2024; it is always worthwhile to call ahead to confirm availability or opening hours.

Ferry information

A number of trips in this book include ferry crossings. In most cases, you will bring your motorcycle across on the ferry; in some instances, you will leave it in a designated parking lot while you explore the coast or isolated communities on foot.

In all cases, check for the most up-to-date schedules and consider making reservations, when possible. Ferry information is accessible through the provincial government's website 511nl.com. On the 511nl homepage, click the box beside "ferries" in the right-hand navigation pane, then navigate to the area of the province in which you are travelling. You may also call 511 for information; if you are outside the province, call 1-833-616-5511 (instructions current as of 2024).

My bikes

Cruisers, tourers, sports bikes, adventure bikes, spiders, and trikes all cruise Newfoundland's highways. I have owned dual-sport bikes capable of driving on- or off-road, such as the 2015 Honda CRF 250L. This bike was appropriate on the provincial trailways but challenging when sharing a highway with an 18-wheeler tractor trailer—I don't recommend it for long days on the highway.

I have owned two Honda Cruisers, including a 750 cc Honda, an ideal choice for long days, especially after I installed a back rest. I installed an extra light bar and back rest on my 1100 cc Honda Cruiser, a better fit for my frame and the highways. My first touring bike was a 1300 cc Yamaha Royal Star Venture, comfortable for long days on the road.

Plan your trip with the assistance of the Newfoundland and Labrador tourism website www.newfoundlandlabrador.com. Tourist information centres along the TCH stock annual Travellers Guide handbooks, which provide accommodation and community event information.

Newfoundland and Labrador's history includes the presence and contributions of Indigenous groups: Paleo-Eskimo, Innu, Inuit, Beothuk, and Mi'kmaq. Many European explorers and fishers came (and settled) from England, Ireland, Portugal, Spain, Italy, Scotland, and Greenland. As you tour Newfoundland, you will learn more about its complex history and rich culture. Let's get at it!

2015 Honda CRF 250L.
My bikes are kept indoors in the winter
and in a bike barn in the summer.
750 cc Honda Cruiser.
1300 cc Yamaha touring bike.
1100 cc Honda Cruiser.
Extra LED light bar installed
on the Honda 1100.

A fishing shed in Diamond Cove.

1 Southwestern Newfoundland, Route 470

Channel-Port aux Basques to Rose Blanche-Harbour Le Cou

> **Distance:** 102 km
>> **Primary road(s):** Route 470
>>> **Amenities:** Channel-Port aux Basques, Isle aux Morts, Rose Blanche

Instead of heading along the TCH as so many do when they drive off the ferry, head east and treat yourself to an afternoon enjoying the scenery and culture of the southwest coast. Riding through the fishing communities hugging the coast along the Cabot Strait is like riding through history. This return trip from Channel-Port aux Basques to Rose Blanche-Harbour Le Cou takes about 2 hours in favourable conditions.

A visitor information centre in Channel-Port aux Basques offers a wealth of information about the area and the province; visit it before heading to Route 470, a coastal road winding in and out of six communities.

About 9 kilometres outside Channel-Port aux Basques heading east along Route 470 is the exit to Margaree and Fox Roost. Leave Route 470 and head south along the Margaree/Fox Roost Road. The communities are well marked by signs along the highway.

In Margaree, view the Atlantic Ocean through the eyes of generations of fishers who have made a living there. In the summer, Margaree Outfitters offers cod jigging tours, sightseeing, and catch-and-release shark fishing.

Just down the road is Fox Roost, a sheltered cove filled with wharves and sheds. Residents are adept at designing sheds that, although they are balanced on a series of stilts, have stood the test of weather and time.

Ride back to Route 470 and head eastward to Isle

Fox Roost harbour.

aux Morts (population 500). The history of some of the shipwrecks, such as *The Rankin*, along this treacherous shoreline, as well as stories of daring rescues made by the local people, are detailed on plaques on well-maintained walking trails and in the community museum. Ann Harvey's family and their Newfoundland dog, Hairyman, rescued almost 200 souls in two daring rescues in the early 1800s; her heroism is celebrated every year during Ann Harvey Days, a 4-day summer festival in late July.

From Isle aux Morts, ride east for 12 kilometres along Route 470 toward Burnt Islands, situated in God Bay: a causeway joins both parts of the community. Fishing families have lived in Burnt Islands since the 1830s.

At the end of Route 470 is Rose Blanche-Harbour Le Cou. The community of Harbour Le Cou is immortalized by Newfoundland singer Dick Nolan:

It was only a motorcycle but it felt like a mode of being.

—Rachel Kushner, *The Flamethrowers*

Margaree, Cabot Strait.

Rose Blanche.

So come all you young sailors
who walk on the shore
Beware of old comrades
you sailed with before
Beware of the maidens with
the bonnets of blue
And the pretty young damsels
of Harbour Le Cou

Rose Blanche-Harbour Le Cou (population 300) is home to Rose Blanche Lighthouse. This community has two well-protected harbours and a rocky coastline. It is protected from the sea by Caines Island and Rose Blanche Point. The lighthouse, built in 1871 with stone from a nearby granite quarry, was restored in 1999.

From Rose Blanche, take the ferry along the coast to

the remote community of La Poile, 1.5 hours away over a distance of 35 kilometres. This ferry does not carry vehicles; for schedules and fees, check www.gov.nl.ca/ti/ferryservices/schedules/k-lapoile/.

Head from the lighthouse to Harbour Le Cou, where frequent fog highlights the need for the lighthouse. Take Route 470 back along the coast to Channel-Port aux Basques.

★ **NOTE: Post-Tropical Storm Fiona**

In September 2022, post-tropical storm Fiona ripped through Eastern Canada. The southwestern part of the island of Newfoundland witnessed great destruction, including along this route. Communities from Port aux Basques to Rose Blanche-Harbour Le Cou experienced extensive damage. The photos in this chapter were taken pre-Fiona; the look of these towns will change as they rebuild.

One of Rose Blanche's protected harbours.

Harbour Le Cou.

Codroy Valley.

CAPE ANGUILLE
406
MILLVILLE
DOYLES
TOMPKINS
407
ST. ANDREW'S
1
CAPE RAY
408
PORT AUX BASQUES
Grand Codroy River
Little Codroy River
Grand Bay River

② Codroy Valley
Channel–Port aux Basques to Cape Anguille

> **Distance:** 135 km
>> **Primary road(s):** TCH; Routes 406, 407, 408
>>> **Amenities:** Channel–Port aux Basques, Doyles

This area of Newfoundland attracts adventure tourists and birdwatchers—this is a stopover for such migratory birds as the endangered piping plover. Many migratory and local birds find shelter and food in the Codroy Valley International Wetlands. Cape Anguille's lighthouse is the most westerly point of the island of Newfoundland.

This 135-kilometre ride starts in the west: Ride from Channel-Port aux Basques on the TCH toward Tompkins; exit left into the Codroy Valley and to Cape Anguille before returning through the valley and heading back to Channel-Port aux Basques from Doyles.

Before leaving Channel-Port aux Basques, ensure that the winds are not raging in the Wreckhouse, near the mouth of the Codroy Valley. Wreckhouse winds are famously fierce and capable of overturning tractor trailers. A large highway billboard at the Port aux Basques tourist information site warns truckers of winds over 80 kilometres/hour. I have left the province at least 15 times on motorcycle and only once have I been advised to take a hotel.

Heading west on the TCH from Channel-Port aux Basques, watch for a sign to the J.T. Cheeseman Park on the left. A short ride over pavement and a graded gravel road leads to the park, which is ideal for camping or sightseeing the Cape Ray beaches and barrens. The park offers angling and beachcombing; cycling, hiking, kayaking, and canoeing are other popular activities.

Return to the TCH and ride 6 kilometres northwest to an exit on the left onto Route 408. Ride 6 more kilometres southeast into Cape Ray (population 350). The 15-metre-high Cape Ray Lighthouse was constructed in the late 1800s.

After relaxing on the beaches of Cape Ray, head northward on the TCH to the exit at Tompkins (population 100). After Tompkins, ride 5 kilometres southwest on Route 407 to St. Andrew's. St. Andrew's na Creige is a privately owned, par 35, 9-hole golf course which boasts views of the Long Range Mountains.

Cape Ray.

This route goes through the Codroy Valley, which starts in the Anguille Mountains and runs along the west coast facing the Gulf of St. Lawrence. The Codroy River flows through the valley toward the gulf. The valley, noted for its farming, was originally settled by the Mi'kmaq and, later, the French, Irish, and Scottish; the latter, from the Scottish Highlands, arrived in the mid-1800s.

From St. Andrew's, ride 7 kilometres northwest through the farming area of Searston toward the Grand Codroy River. After crossing the river, enter the Codroy Valley Provincial

Cape Anguille Lighthouse.

Park and ride northwest to Millville, 4 kilometres away.

Millville's carding mill was set up by Alexander Gale in the 1940s; it later became a museum. The carding mill's machines untangled and cleaned sheep's wool, a process that was used before a more continuous fibre was processed to make wool cloth. On the side of the museum building a sign points toward the Cape Anguille Lighthouse and the Holy Trinity Anglican Church in Codroy, 3 kilometres away.

Cape Anguille is the most westerly point of the island of Newfoundland, an ideal place to construct a lighthouse and fog alarm building overlooking the Gulf of St. Lawrence in 1908. Fifty years later, the buildings were reconstructed.

Leaving the Cape Anguille area, backtrack toward Millville and turn left at the Great Codroy River and ride along the north side of the river, through the Great Codroy Valley.

From the valley, ride south on Route 406 toward Doyles and then follow the TCH south to Channel-Port aux Basques.

J.T. Cheeseman Provincial Park.

St. Andrew's na Creige Golf Course.

Cape Anguille Lighthouse Inn.

Heatherton goats.

3 Bay St. George South

Crabbes River Park to Highlands to Journois

> **Distance:** 173 km
>> **Primary road(s):** TCH; Routes 403, 404, 405
>>> **Amenities:** St. Fintan's, Robinsons, Flat Bay

Locally known as Bay St. George, this area may also appear as Baie St-George or St. George's Bay on maps. Bay St. George is 64 kilometres wide and stretches from Cape Anguille (Codroy Valley) in the south to Cape St. George (Port au Port Peninsula) in the north. This 173-kilometre trip consists of two loops, each of which starts and ends at the TCH.

This route is paved except for 7 kilometres between Heatherton and Fischells. Roads wind along the ocean and through farmlands and communities, with plenty of opportunities for wildlife and bird sightings. If you enjoy salmon fishing and own a licence, pack a rod to fish Crabbes River and Robinsons River or to try your luck for trout in Flat Bay Brook. Hikers have many options too: walk coastal trails alongside the meadows and access lookouts over Bay St. George.

The south loop

From the TCH, turn left onto Route 405. The first landmark to watch for on Route 405 is Station Grocery in St. Fintan's. At the store, turn left toward Highlands along Route 405 (Highlands Road). Highlands' residents have fished and farmed since the 1800s, when people arrived from Ireland and Scotland, many with a Roman Catholic background. St. Columcille Catholic Church was built in Highlands in 1882. Highlands has approximately 100 year-round residents, but

Fishing gear along the Gulf of St. Lawrence.

that number increases in the summer. Walk some of the access trails to the coast to appreciate views of the Gulf.

From Highlands, ride back to St. Fintan's and turn left at Station Grocery to travel northwest along Taylor's Road to the coast. Pass the community of St. David's on the left, then turn onto Maidstone Road.

Stay on the coastal Maidstone Road and ride north toward Jeffrey's. Along the way you pass St. Michael and All Angels Anglican Church on the left. Beyond it is a bridge from which you can see boats and fishing gear.

About 5 kilometres farther along the road is Robinsons. Instead of exiting on Route 404 at Robinsons toward the TCH, continue along the coastal road to Heatherton (farming country) and Fischells (a fishing community). These two communities are easy to access, but the last section of road into Fischells is a gravel road.

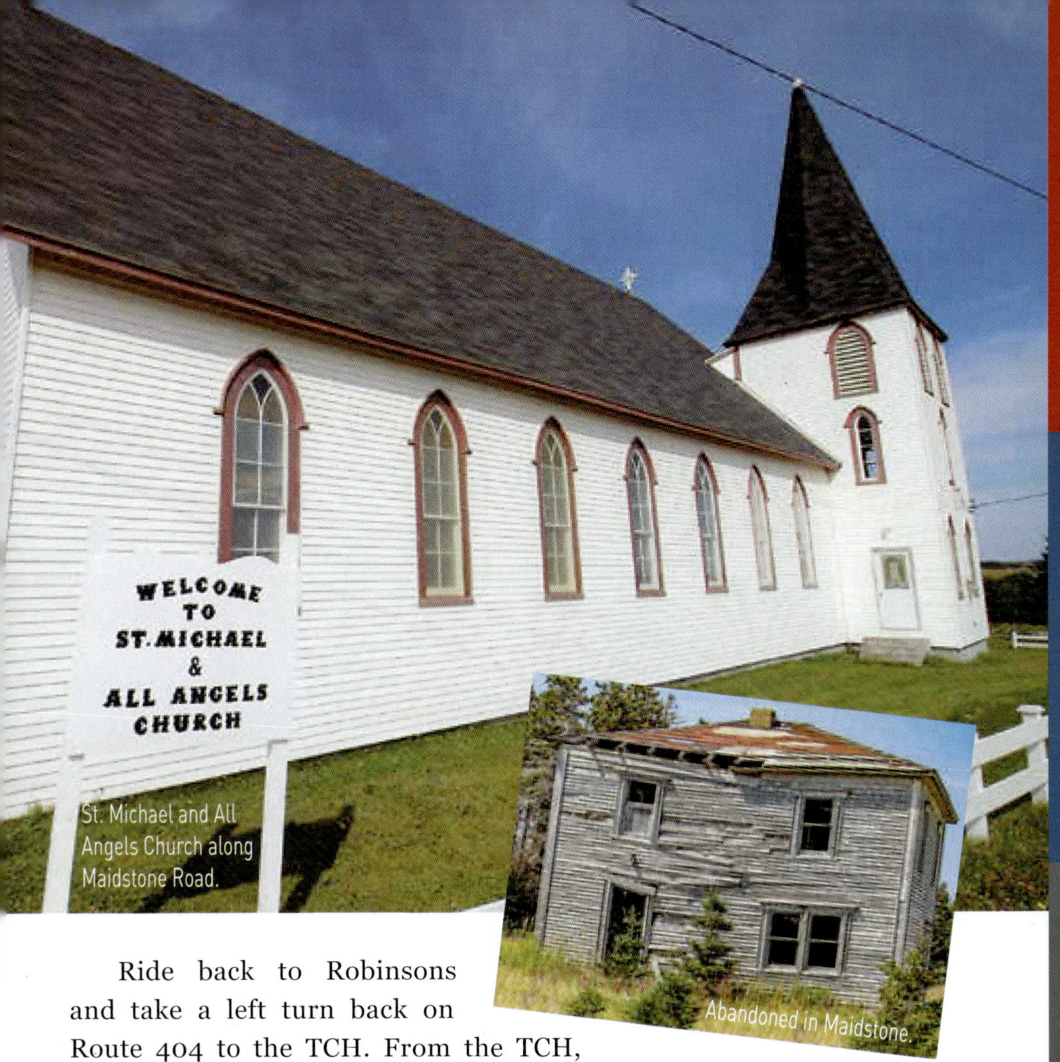

St. Michael and All Angels Church along Maidstone Road.

Abandoned in Maidstone.

Ride back to Robinsons and take a left turn back on Route 404 to the TCH. From the TCH, head south on the TCH back to Crabbes River Park or continue on to the north loop toward Flat Bay and Journois.

The north loop

To complete the north loop, head northeast on the TCH for about 27 kilometres until you see Route 403 heading to the left. This takes you to Flat Bay, Flat Bay West, St. Teresa, and Journois.

Flat Bay, or Epwikek, is a Mi'kmaq community with a population of 200. The Mi'kmaq were here as early as the 1760s and traded with Europeans who came to the area. Mi'kmaq descendants still live in this area. At Flat Bay, leave the coast and head back on Route 403 to the TCH. Ride 37 kilometres south to Crabbes River Park to complete this loop.

The cliffs of Cape St. George.
BLACK DUCK BROOK
THREE ROCK COVE
463
WEST BAY
MAINLAND
THE GRAVELS
AGUATHUNA
ABRAHAMS COVE
460
CAMPBELL'S CREEK
CAPE ST. GEORGE

4 Port au Port Peninsula

> **Distance:** 153 km
>> **Primary road(s):** Routes 460, 463
>>> **Amenities:** Stephenville, Port au Port West

Port au Port is a bilingual (French and English) peninsula, west of the town of Stephenville (population 6,600). The main roads trace the peninsula's coastline, passing beaches, cliffs, and pasturelands and travelling through several communities. The peninsula is connected to the mainland by a narrow isthmus near the town of Port au Port.

To get to the peninsula, from the TCH take Route 460 through Stephenville. The peninsula entrance is at the Gravels Walking Trail, which marks the beginning of this 153-kilometre loop ride.

As you enter the peninsula along the isthmus in Port au Port West, look for a large parking lot at the right for the Gravels Walking Trail. It's worth walking even part of the trail to see the unusually shaped rocks and small secluded beaches on Port au Port Bay.

From the Gravels Walking Trail, ride northwest, following the road signs along Main Street (which becomes Aguathuna Road) to Our Lady of Mercy Catholic Church, constructed in the early 1900s: the tallest wooden church in the province, at 35 metres.

Continue on Aguathuna Road to the community of Boswarlos for another glimpse of the unusual shoreline.

After this detour, head back to Aguathuna and turn right on Father Joy's Road, just before Our Lady of Mercy Church, and head south onto Route 460. This begins the loop around

Lobster pots in Three Rock Cove.

the peninsula, starting along the southern shoreline toward Cape St. George. The paved coastal road offers views of the bay and its dramatic cliffs. The first community is Campbell's Creek, a farming area. A few minutes later is Abraham's Cove—an ideal place to stop and enjoy the view.

Six kilometres later is Lower Cove and its beautiful cobblestone beach. The official name of the community is Ship Cove-Lower Cove-Jerry's Nose and it is home to a large limestone quarry. Another 5 kilometres brings you to the Sheaves Cove exit. If you are willing to travel less than 1 kilometre on a gravel road, you'll reach the coast and a small fishing area, where tourists are treated to the sight of water crashing on the large rocks and waterfalls in the same cove.

Back on Route 460, head west 12 kilometres to the Mi'kmaq community of De Grau. Just down the road is the Harbour Authority of Cape St. George, a facility used by the people of

De Grau. Next is the community of Cape St. George, best known for cliffs which jut out into the Gulf of St. Lawrence. Boutte du Cap Park, west of the community of Cape St. George, offers views of the hills of Cape St. George—a perfect spot to catch a summer sunset.

Leaving Cape St. George, ride northeast 16 kilometres along the northern side of the peninsula toward Port au Port Bay. From the next community, Mainland, you can see Red Island off its coast. If you're hungry, stop by Tea by the Sea (the fish and chips is delicious).

Another 10 kilometres along the coast is Three Rock Cove, originally Trois Cailloux, named for three eroded rocks

The cliffs of Cape St. George.
Our Lady of Mercy Catholic Church in Aguathuna.
Lower Cove, Port au Port Peninsula.

offshore. Three Rock Cove is a farming community, but stacks of lobster pots attest to its fishing activities.

Next is Lourdes (population 300). The parish, Our Lady of Lourdes, maintains a grotto similar to the site in Lourdes, France. Its grotto was carved by a local stonemason.

Riding northeast on a narrow strip of land from Lourdes takes you to Black Duck Brook, the birthplace of fiddler Émile Benoît, nestled in a cove surrounded by high cliffs.

Backtrack to Lourdes, then take Route 463 south to Abraham's Cove and on to Route 460, passing through West Bay and Piccadilly, and back to the Gravels Walking Trail, ending a spectacular ride. This ride can be done in 3 hours, but I recommend spending a day on the peninsula.

Sandbanks Park.
BARACHOIS POND
PROVINCIAL PARK
480
BURGEO
GREY RIVER
FRANÇOIS
RAMEA

⑤ Burgeo plus Ferries

> **Distance:** 306 km
>> **Primary road(s):** Route 480 (Burgeo Highway)
>>> **Amenities:** Burgeo

This trip takes you down the Burgeo Highway to isolated Burgeo and its pristine sandy beaches and offers an opportunity to explore part of Newfoundland's south coast by ferry.

The 150-kilometre highway—Route 480, also known as Burgeo Road and sometimes the Caribou Trail—intersects with the TCH near Barachois Pond Provincial Park. The Burgeo Highway passes through the Annieopsquotch Mountains, as well as through barren tundra, marshlands, and forests. The paved road winds through a landscape devoid of any towns— you will pass hunting cabins and camps but no amenities until Burgeo. Until the highway was constructed in 1971, the only way to get to the town was by ferry.

About 50 kilometres along the highway is a turnoff to Buchans; that route is poorly maintained and not suggested for cruising on a motorcycle.

The Burgeo Highway is known for frequent moose and caribou sightings. If you can, ride on a sunny day for safety and to appreciate the grandeur of the landscape.

On the approach to Burgeo is the entrance to Sandbanks Provincial Park. Relatively flat and well-maintained shore walks and trails offer excellent access to the park's 7 kilometres of soft, sandy beaches. Walk the first major beach to reach Cow Head, a viewing area. Sandbanks is one of the wonders of the province. Naturalists and authors Farley and Claire Mowat wrote about this area, and artist Christopher

Waterway into Grey River.

American sailboat leaving Burgeo.

Francois.

Burgeo.

Pratt painted here. It is a popular destination for campers, canoeists, kayakers, photographers, and naturalists.

Burgeo (population 1,176) is 3 kilometres from the park. As you enter the town, you'll see a wooden stairway that leads up Maiden Tea Hill to a view of Burgeo and Grandy Island. Burgeo encompasses a number of bridges and causeways—within 8 kilometres of Burgeo are 365 islands. You'll see plenty of evidence of the fishing industry that is the heart of this town.

Burgeo has restaurants, grocery stores, gas stations, and accommodations (book a place to stay before you ride all the way to this southern town).

From the Burgeo ferry terminal, you can travel to three communities (Ramea, Grey River, and Francois) that can only be accessed by boat. There is no need for a bike in the island community of Ramea but you can, technically, take your bike across on the ferry. Grey River and Francois do not have vehicle roads, and walking is the preferred mode of travel. Check the ferry schedules from Burgeo to these remote communities ahead of time, as the ferries do not run every day (call 1-833-NLFERRY or 709-729-3835).

This ferry system goes farther east to McCallum, Gaultois, and Hermitage but these communities are easier to access from the Connaigre Peninsula (Trip 23).

Travel on these provincial ferries is inexpensive. Accommodations are available in Ramea or Francois; no official accommodations are available in Grey River but a Facebook query or a call to the town hall may connect you to a local resident offering accommodations.

The closest community to Burgeo is Ramea on Northwest Island. A gentle 7-kilometre walking trail leads around Ramea, taking you to windmills, a lighthouse, and endless ocean views. From Ramea, the ferry travels to Grey River (population 200). A tungsten mine and sawmill are operational but fishing has long been the primary industry in the area. If you have time, walk to the lookout above Grey River to appreciate the fjord and the protected community.

A hunting lodge operates in one of the southern fjords just outside Grey River. We paid for the gas and time for a local resident to take us up that spectacular fjord via boat.

Farther down the south coast, the ferry enters another fjord to get to Francois. Like Grey River, Francois is nestled in a harbour well protected by the walls of the fjord and the mountains behind the community. From the large hill, called The Friar, behind Francois, you will see few trees or land that can be farmed; it is obvious why fishing sustained this community. Residents make good use of the available space in Francois for houses, wharves, walkways, and gardens.

A visit to Burgeo, Ramea, Grey River, and Francois could turn into a three- to four-day adventure. I have done it and will remember it forever.

Between Grey River and Francois.

View of Burgeo from Maiden Tea Hill.

Good use of the land in Francois.

Bottle Cove.

BOTTLE COVE
LARK HARBOUR
YORK HARBOUR
450
JOHN'S BEACH
HALFWAY POINT
MOUNT MORIAH
CURLING
CORNER BROOK

Bay of Islands South

> **Distance:** 100 km
>> **Primary road(s):** Route 450
>>> **Amenities:** Corner Brook

This 100-kilometre return trip follows the south side of the Bay of Islands from Corner Brook to Lark Harbour, with a diversion to Bottle Cove. Combine this ride with Trip 7 for a full day out.

Corner Brook (population 31,000), on the Bay of Islands at the mouth of the Humber River, is a playground for outdoor enthusiasts, with opportunities for skiing, kayaking, canoeing, mountain biking, and running. Cruise ships also use the port. Stop at the Newfoundland Emporium, which sells locally made jams and candies and souvenirs, postcards, art, crafts, antiques, and books.

From Corner Brook, head west on the Lewin Parkway to Curling. Once a fishing community, Curling is now a mostly residential neighbourhood of Corner Brook.

From Curling, ride about 4 kilometres northwest along Route 450 to Mount Moriah (population 700) at Humber Mouth. From this community is a view back into Corner Brook.

Throughout the Bay of Islands, many of the fishing boats are painted orange. I asked an area fisher why that was the case. His response: "There is one can of paint in the Bay of Islands and we all use it."

Continue on Route 450 to Benoit's Cove and then to John's Beach. On a sunny afternoon, you may see a Kruger paper boat heading out the Bay of Islands transporting some of the 200,000 tonnes of newsprint the company's Corner Brook Pulp and Paper mill produces each year. At the mill, nine

Paper boat passing by St. Ambrose Anglican Church in John's Beach.

York Harbour.

The Bay of Islands is an inlet northwest of Corner Brook. A sub-basin of the Gulf of St. Lawrence, the Bay of Islands is surrounded by the Long Range Mountains and is a drainage area for the Humber River as it leaves Deer Lake. When operational, Corner Brook's pulp and paper mill uses the Bay of Islands waterways to export its products.

The Bay of Islands is between Lewis Hills on the south and the Tablelands on the north. The largest island in the Bay of Islands is Woods Island at the head of the bay.

generators produce 138 megawatts of energy by managing the large reservoir in the nearby town of Deer Lake.

As you continue along Route 450, you'll enjoy views of the bay and the Long Range Mountains, which surround the Bay of Islands. Humber Arm South day park in Frenchman's Cove is a good spot to stop to admire the view and capture some photos. The island offshore in Frenchman's Cove is called Guernsey Island but residents call it Wee Ball.

Ride another 16 kilometres along Route 450 to York Harbour-Lark Harbour. Captain James Cook surveyed

Sacred Heart Church in Curling.

this coast in the 1700s aboard the HMS *York* and HMS *Lark*, giving the communities their names. These scenic towns have amazing views, day parks, whale watching and fishing (in season), accommodations, and restaurants. Walking trails include the OBIEC (Outer Bay of Islands Enhancement Committee) Copper Mine Falls Trail by York Harbour and the Blow Me Down Trail. Both are well marked and well used.

Blow Me Down Provincial Park, situated between York Harbour and Lark Harbour, has 28 campsites.

From Lark Harbour, ride 3 kilometres in a northwesterly direction along Little Port Road to Bottle Cove with its colourful, busy harbour. Get off your bike and stroll among the caves and cliffs; the area also has many boardwalks and paths.

From here, it takes another hour or so to bike the 50 kilometres back to Corner Brook.

Gillams. Note the snow on the mountains across the bay.

⑦ Bay of Islands North

> **Distance:** 114 km
>> **Primary road(s):** TCH; Route 440
>>> **Amenities:** Cox's Cove, Marble Mountain Ski Resort, Corner Brook

This trip along the north side of the Bay of Islands takes you from Little Rapids, approximately 25 kilometres east of Corner Brook, to Cox's Cove and back to Little Rapids.

Little Rapids, population 225, is predominantly farm country. As you approach Little Rapids from Corner Brook along the TCH, stop by the Greenhouse and Garden Store to appreciate local shrubs and plants.

Continue southwest along the TCH to Steady Brook, the community nearest Marble Mountain Ski Resort. The resort is on the slopes of the Humber River Valley about 7 kilometres east of Corner Brook and receives up to 20 feet of natural snow in a winter. Its detachable lift rises 1,660 metres and takes 7 minutes to ride.

Marble Mountain also has a zipline operation, Marble Zip Tours. From the zipline are spectacular views of Humber Valley and Marble Mountain Resort. Accommodations and restaurants are available near Marble Mountain and in Corner Brook. In the summer, hiking and biking trails, kayaking, and canoeing attract tourists.

Ride south along the TCH from Steady Brook and Marble Mountain and take the exit to Route 440 to Bay of Islands North. You will cross a small bridge to the right within a minute or so of getting on Route 440. After passing through Hughes Brook (population 200+), continue to Irishtown-Summerside. The south side of the Bay of Islands is visible

Fishers in McIvers.

from here; on a clear day, you may spot smoke from the Kruger Pulp and Paper Mill in Corner Brook.

Continue on Route 440 along the coastline to Meadows (population 400) and enjoy a view of the Long Range Mountains across the water.

Head north on Route 440 to Gillams. An orange dory with green trim and an anchor, floats, buoys, and crab pot at the outskirts of town is an eye-catching display. A dory, a boat with a V-shaped stern with a narrow, flat bottom, is a common sight in Newfoundland. Dories can be rowed, sailed, or engine-powered.

About 8 kilometres farther along Route 440 is the fishing community of McIvers (population 575). In McIvers, I left the main road and took a short gravel road for a closer look at the cove of McIvers. I chatted with residents as they were splitting cod on the wharf.

From McIvers, Route 440 takes a turn northeast across the final peninsula of the Bay of Islands to Cox's Cove. This fishing and logging town (population 600+), was settled by herring and lobster fishers. Incorporated in 1969, it hosts the Big Hill Festival each summer. Accommodations, restaurants, walking trails, and adventure boat tours are available.

From Cox's Cove, travel directly back to Little Rapids or explore more of the Bay of Islands as you return.

Cox's Cove.
Marble Mountain, Steady Brook.
Marble Mountain, Steady Brook.
McIvers.

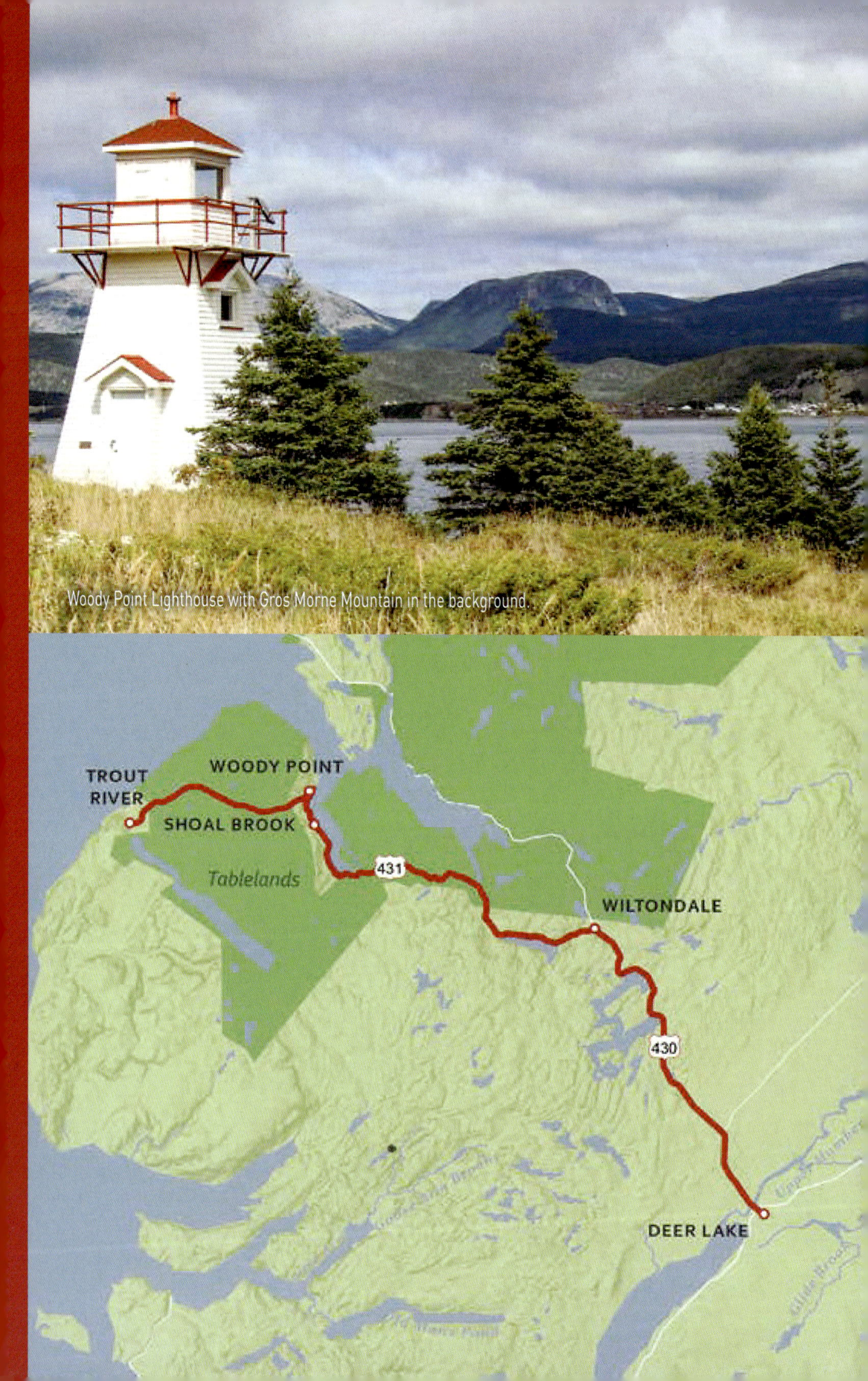

Woody Point Lighthouse with Gros Morne Mountain in the background.

8 Deer Lake to Trout River
TCH to Gros Morne National Park

> **Distance:** 164 km
>> **Primary road(s):** Routes 430, 431
>>> **Amenities:** Wiltondale, Woody Point, Trout River, Deer Lake

Trip 8 is a leisurely 164-kilometre return ride from Deer Lake to Trout River. From the Deer Lake Irving Big Stop Restaurant on the TCH, take Route 430 (The Viking Trail); at the northern tip of the Great Northern Peninsula (434 kilometres from Deer Lake) is the L'Anse aux Meadows National Historic Site, where Vikings landed 1,000 years ago.

Take Route 430 to Reidville for a stop at the Newfoundland Insectarium, visible from Route 430. This fascinating educational centre, open from May to the fall, houses a butterfly garden, as well as thousands of insects, arachnids, and arthropods.

Route 430 leads northward on paved highways all the way to L'Anse aux Meadows—but this trip leaves the route at Wiltondale, 29 kilometres north of the Insectarium. As you ride toward Wiltondale, you will appreciate the hills and bodies of water such as Bonne Bay Big Pond. Wiltondale marks the entrance to Gros Morne National Park and an opportunity to purchase gas, liquor, and food. Wiltondale is named for its first settler, Norman Wilton, who moved to the area in 1927 to provide a way station for logging and sawmill operations. Later, with the opening of Gros Morne National

Socks for sale in Trout River.

Park, tourism became the main source of employment.

At Wiltondale is the intersection of Routes 430 and 431. Turn left onto Route 431 and ride 30 kilometres, through the communities of Glenburnie and Birchy Head, to Shoal Brook, which is located on South Arm. Shoal Brook is on the southern section of Gros Morne National Park. Camping is available at Water's Edge RV Park and Campground in Shoal Brook. From here you can enjoy all the attractions of Bonne Bay.

Four kilometres north of Shoal Brook is the tourist town of Woody Point (population 300) on Bonne Bay. The town is made up of Curzon Village, Woody Point, and Winterhouse

Brook. Woody Point Lighthouse was built in 1919. Woody Point is also well known for its churches, fine arts centres, restaurants, and access to the Gros Morne National Park Discovery Centre.

Across the bay from Woody Point is Norris Point, accessible by a 15-minute ferry ride from Woody Point. This is convenient for visitors to the cultural events of Writers at Woody Point and the Gros Morne Summer Music Festival.

Gros Morne's world-class trails include the Tablelands and Green Garden Trail. In the Tablelands, you can walk on rock that was once the Earth's mantle.

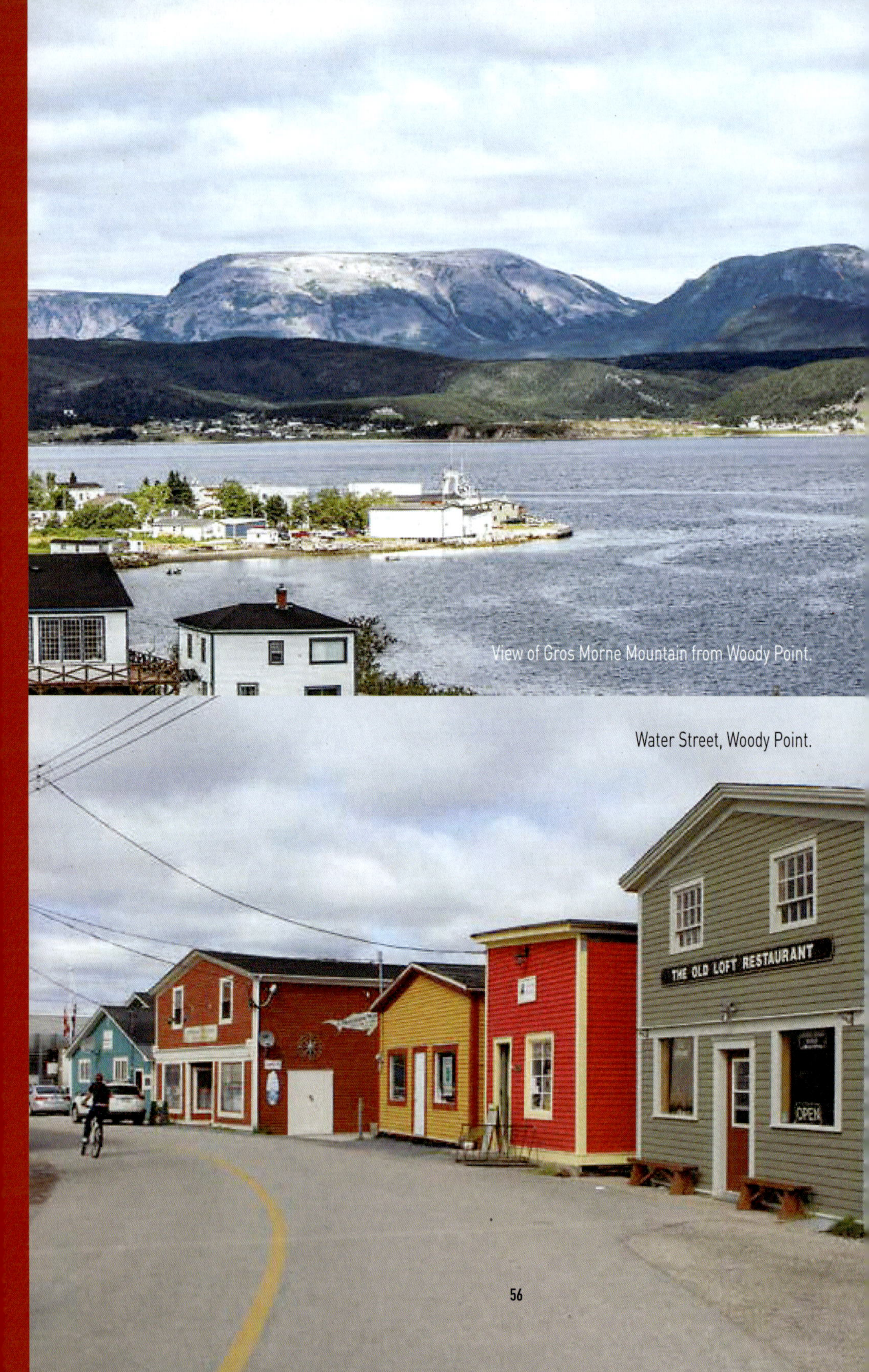

View of Gros Morne Mountain from Woody Point.

Water Street, Woody Point.

The Tablelands.

Backtrack from Woody Point along Route 431 to the Bonne Bay Inn; turn toward the Tablelands and Trout River. As it can be very windy on motorcycle along this route, ride with caution. About 5 kilometres along the road, you'll see the otherworldly landscape of the Tablelands. A 4-kilometre trail winds along an old seabed around a mountain that has been pushed to the surface from colliding continents millions of years ago.

Twelve kilometres farther on the road is the end of Route 431 in Trout River, a fishing village settled in 1815 by the George Crocker family and known today for its boardwalk and sunset views.

After exploring the insectarium, Wiltondale, Shoal Brook, Woody Point, the Tablelands, and Trout River, you can wind your way back 82 kilometres to Deer Lake.

View from Martin's Point

COW HEAD
ST. PAULS
WESTERN BROOK POND TRAIL
SALLY'S COVE
430
ROCKY HARBOUR
NORRIS POINT
WILTONDALE

9 Gros Morne National Park

Wiltondale to Cow Head

> **Distance:** 181 km
>> **Primary road(s):** Route 430
>>> **Amenities:** Wiltondale, Rocky Harbour

This trip leads through the northern part of Gros Morne National Park, north of Wiltondale to Cow Head. Route 430 through the park is in excellent condition (as of 2024) and the scenery is spectacular. Accommodations, restaurants, and other amenities are readily available; however, since you will likely be travelling this area in the summer, book hotels, campgrounds, festivals, and dining rooms in advance.

From Wiltondale take Route 430 north toward Cow Head. After riding approximately 34 kilometres, take a left turn toward Norris Point. This spectacular ride offers views of Bonne Bay on the left and mountains on the right.

Norris Point is named for an original settler, Neddy Norris, who arrived in the late 1700s with his family. Later on, people from England, Ireland, and Scotland came to the area to fish in the fall herring fishery. They were also interested in the lobster fishery and fur trapping.

Leaving Norris Point on Route 430 offers a view of Gros Morne Mountain, the highest peak on the west coast. The hike up the mountain is a full day's trek and is challenging but worthwhile.

A stop in Rocky Harbour is a must for people visiting Gros Morne National Park. From

Western Brook Pond tour boat.

Animals travel on all fours. Mankind on two. Motorcycling is not a means of transport but an ideology, a nomadic way of life.

—Amit Reddy

Norris Point, ride to Rocky Harbour one of two ways: turn left into the town along Harbour Drive; or leave Norris Point on Pond Road, which runs parallel to Route 430 and also leads to Rocky Harbour.

Originally known as Small Bay or Little Harbour, Rocky Harbour (population 950) is the most populous community in the park.

The Rocky Harbour area is a hub for tourist activities, including boat tours with Bon Tours (music, cod jigging, sunset cruises, and educational tours are available), craft

shops, restaurants, and music and comedy shows. A short ride from Rocky Harbour leads to Lobster Cove Head Lighthouse and walking trails along the coast and through old tuckamore forests, which have been stunted by winds and the ravages of winter storms.

From Rocky Harbour, ride along the ocean's edge north on Route 430 to Sally's Cove and Martin's Point (where remnants of SS *Ethie*, shipwrecked in 1919, are visible). Just past Martin's Point is the large parking lot for the Western Brook Pond Trail.

Western Brook Pond.

The Western Brook Pond experience is like no other in the park. This 16-kilometre-long landlocked fjord created by glaciers offers wildlife, waterfalls, clear water, and the steep cliffs of the Long Range Mountains. Park your motorcycle in the lot and walk about 45 minutes to the tour-boat launch on Western Brook Pond; the boat tour is a must-do.

Back on Road 430, head toward St. Pauls, known as *Uapashku Napaue* by the Innu, a fishing community of 200 surrounded by the Long Range Mountains. Close by St. Pauls inlet is the Gros Morne Golf Course.

Past St. Pauls is Cow Head, the final community at the head of Gros Morne National Park. It boasts a long sandy beach and unobstructed views of the Long Range Mountains. Cow Head (population 400) is home to the Gros Morne Theatre Festival, hosted by Theatre Newfoundland and Labrador.

From Cow Head, it's an 84-kilometre ride south back to Wiltondale.

Gros Morne.

Bonne Bay Marine Station and public aquarium in Norris Point.

Arches Provincial Park.
PORT AU CHOIX
PORT SAUNDERS
HAWKES BAY
RIVER OF PONDS
430
DANIEL'S HARBOUR
PORTLAND CREEK
THE ARCHES PROVINCIAL PARK
PARSONS POND
THREE MILE ROCK

10 Great Northern Peninsula North of Gros Morne National Park

Three Mile Rock to Port au Choix

> **Distance:** 218 km
>> **Primary road(s):** Route 430
>>> **Amenities:** Parson's Pond, Hawke's Bay, River of Ponds, Port Saunders, Port au Choix

The views along this route are spectacular and the ocean is powerful—and so is the wind. The vegetation exemplifies nature's power: bent trees and shores being battered by surf.

In past winters, residents of Parson's Pond travelled 3 miles south to fish at a place with a large rock; they named this fishing region Three Mile Rock. Samuel and Catherine Payne were its first settlers and fishers; it is still a fishing community. Three Mile Rock has a small parking and viewing area for visitors to see the magnificent Great Northern Peninsula and the Gulf of St. Lawrence.

Songwriter Stan Rogers wrote about the *Mary Ellen Carter* that sank off Three Mile Rock:

> *She went down last October*
> *in a pouring rain*
> *The skipper, he's been drinking*
> *and the Mate, he felt no pain*
> *Too close to Three Mile Rock,*
> *and she was dealt her mortal blow*
> *And the* Mary Ellen Carter
> *settled low.*

Ride north on Route 430 to Parson's Pond, a fishing community and, given its natural beauty and proximity to Cow Head and Gros Morne National Park, a popular tourist accommodation

Cod drying on flakes, Port au Choix.

hub. It's also been the site of oil exploration through the decades.

About 10 kilometres north of Parson's Pond is Arches Provincial Park near the Portland Creek area, with a boardwalk and a picnic area overlooking the photogenic arches carved by tidal erosion. The Arches are, without a doubt, a geological curiosity. The smooth beach stones are easy to traverse even when wearing motorcycle boots.

As you continue along Route 430, the waves of the Gulf of St. Lawrence are visible on the left all the way to Daniel's Harbour; watch for whales. The wind here can be challenging as well as exhilarating on a motorcycle; mostly, it is the latter.

A zinc mine was operational in Daniel's Harbour (population 220) until 1990. The community is also home to the Nurse Myra Bennett Heritage House. Bennett, an English nurse and midwife who came to Newfoundland in 1921, at the age of 31, is said to have delivered over 5,000 babies in this province. (A performance theatre in Cow Head, Nurse Myra Bennett Centre for the Performing Arts, opened in 2021.)

Ben's Studio, Port au Choix.

Daniel's Harbour is also the birthplace of Rufus Guinchard, a renowned Newfoundland fiddle player, accordionist, and composer. Guinchard, born in 1899 in Daniel's Harbour, lived in Hawke's Bay farther up the coast until he was 91.

From Daniel's Harbour, continue north, with the Gulf's shoreline on the left and the Long Range Mountains on the right. Three kilometres past the fishing community of Bellburns is Table Point Ecological Reserve, home to fossils and rocks documenting the changes on the continental shelf of the Atlantic Ocean. Park your bike off the highway and walk to this wonder, which dates back 460 million years; no bikes or cars are allowed in this preserve.

Continue 23 kilometres northeast on Route 430 to River of Ponds, an ideal place to stop for gas, food, or a night in River of Ponds Campground or Riverside Chalets. The area boasts walking trails and salmon fishing and you can never discount the amazing views available in all directions.

Hawke's Bay is 19 kilometres northeast along Route 430. Visit the Torrent River Salmon Interpretation Centre

Riding toward Daniel's Harbour.

Port au Choix.

and Fishway. The Torrent River Inn is popular with anglers, hunters, snowmobilers, and outdoor hikers because of its location and its modern facilities

Continue 8 kilometres and turn left onto Route 430-28 to Port Saunders and Port au Choix. Port Saunders (population 678) is named for British admiral Saunders. This well-protected harbour has a long history associated with the marine and fishing industries. French settlers also fished in this area. In the mid-1900s, the area's first fish plant was built. The Port Saunders historic waterfront is home to an operational marine service centre.

Port au Choix is a Parks Canada National Historic Site. Fishers have been coming to this part of the Great Northern Peninsula for at least 6,000 years. Many Indigenous groups were here long before European settlers, including the Maritime Archaic people, the Dorset people, and the

Port Saunders.

Groswater people, as well as other Indigenous peoples. Sealing and cod fishing have sustained this area for centuries. Explore archaeological finds along limestone barrens, forests, and bays with the guidance of Parks Canada trails and information sites.

Point Riche Lighthouse, also in Port au Choix, is maintained by the Port au Choix National Historic Site. The town is home to three Maritime Archaic cemeteries, where 117 skeletons have been found. The French Rooms Cultural Centre Community Museum & Bread Oven is also in Port au Choix. Its oven is similar to French ovens in Coachman's Cove and Cape St. George.

Leave Port au Choix via Route 430-28 to arrive back at Route 430. Exit right and Route 430 brings you back to Three Mile Rock—this time with the ocean on the right and the mountains on the left.

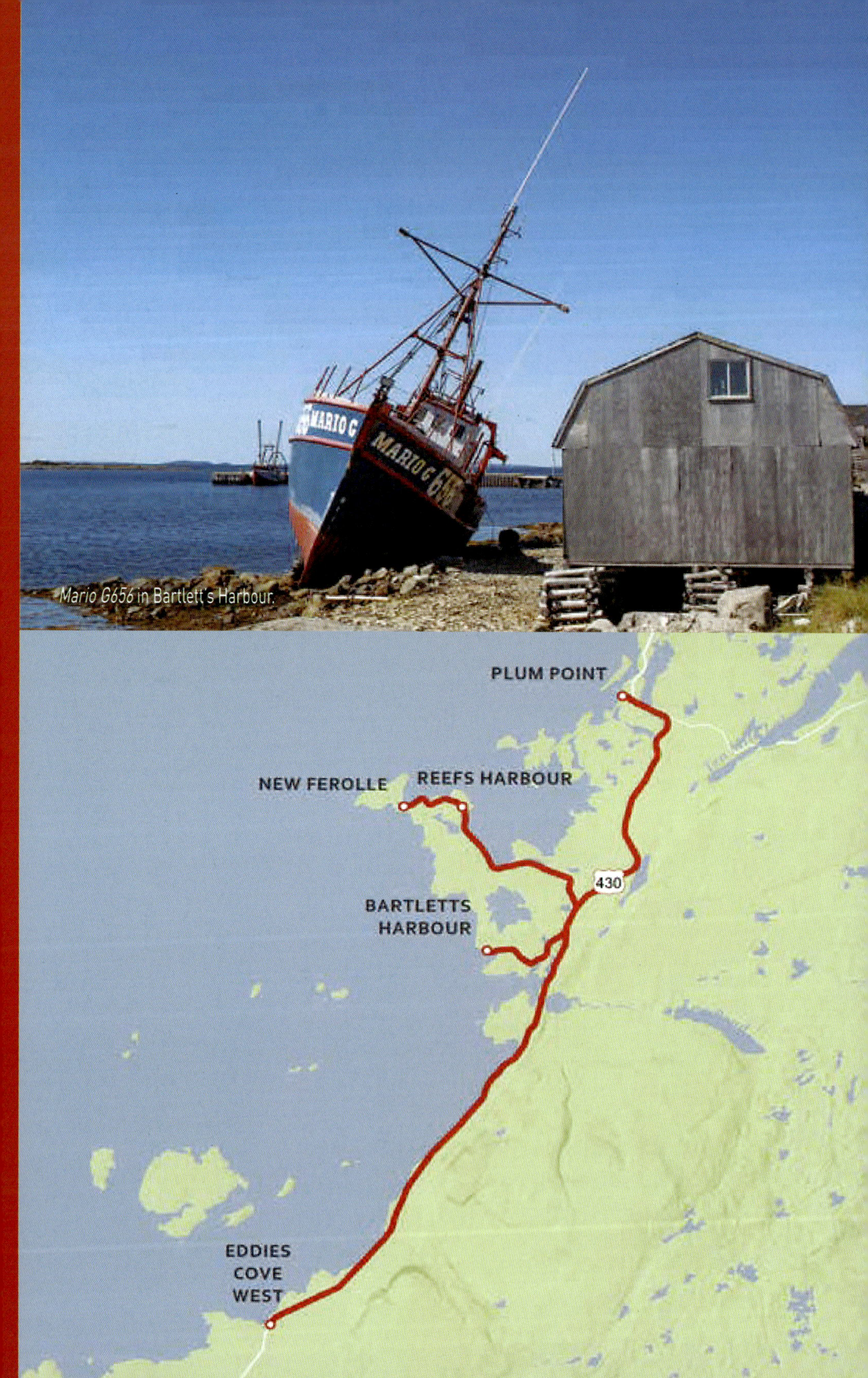

Mario G656 in Bartlett's Harbour.

11

Gros Morne Coast
Eddies Cove West to Plum Point

> **Distance:** 141 km
>> **Primary road(s):** Route 430
>>> **Amenities:** Plum Point

Trip 11 takes you from Eddies Cove West on Route 430 (The Viking Trail) to Plum Point and back.

Eddies Cove West is a fishing village (population 36) in St. John Bay on the Great Northern Peninsula. The largest of the four islands just off Eddies Cove West is St. John Island.

From Eddies Cove West, head north on Route 430 toward Bartlett's Harbour, 35 kilometres away. En route, you'll cross Castor River, one of the premier salmon and sea trout rivers on the Great Northern Peninsula. Two very small communities, Castor River North and South, are on either side of the mouth of the Castor River.

After crossing the bridge at the mouth of the river, watch for a road on the left (Route 430-32) into Bartlett's Harbour, a fishing community of about 130 residents nestled around a rocky, shallow inlet. The abandoned fishing vessel *Mario G656* sits in the inlet, listing to its port side.

Return to Route 430. Approximately 2 kilometres north is the left turn onto Reef's Harbour Road (430-36). As of 2024, the roads are well maintained and pleasant to ride on.

Reef's Harbour-Shoal Cove West-New Ferolle has a combined population of 100. In the area, you may note firewood being stored teepee style to facilitate drying; this style of wood storage is also common on the Labrador coast. Vegetable gardens along the side of the highways are also a frequent sight in this area.

Route 430 heading north to Eddies Cove West.

Boardwalk behind Plum Point Motel.

New Ferolle is 3 kilometres west of Reef's Harbour along 430-36 (Reef's Harbour Road). New Ferolle Lighthouse, located on the Ferolle Peninsula on the Strait of Belle Isle separating St. Margaret's Bay from St. John Bay, was built in 1912; it became automated in 1992.

Backtrack to Route 430 and head north to Plum Point. For one more picturesque diversion, travel southwest off Route 430 just before Plum Point for 5 kilometres to reach Brig Bay and Bird Cove.

Brig Bay and Bird Cove

Brig Bay's protected harbour was mapped by Captain James Cook in 1764. A brig is a sailing ship. As Darby's Island shelters the harbour of Brig Bay, a few ships at a time can moor away from the ocean winds. English, Basque, and French fishers

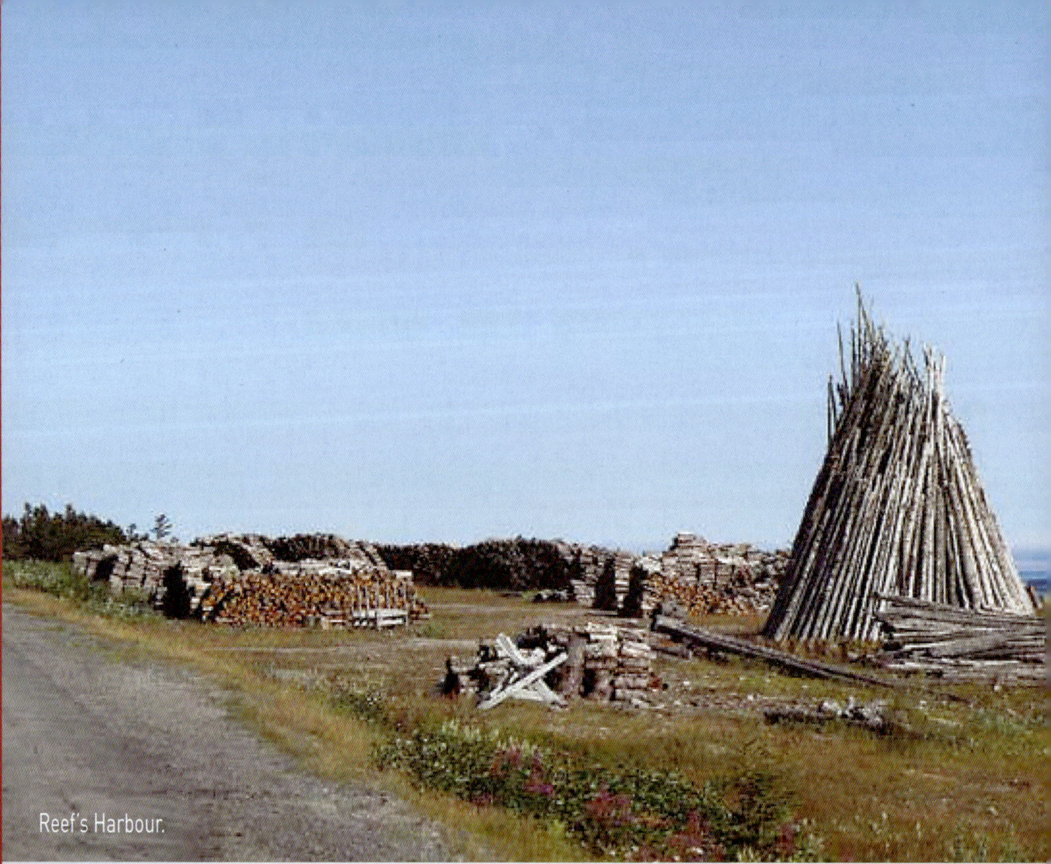
Reef's Harbour.

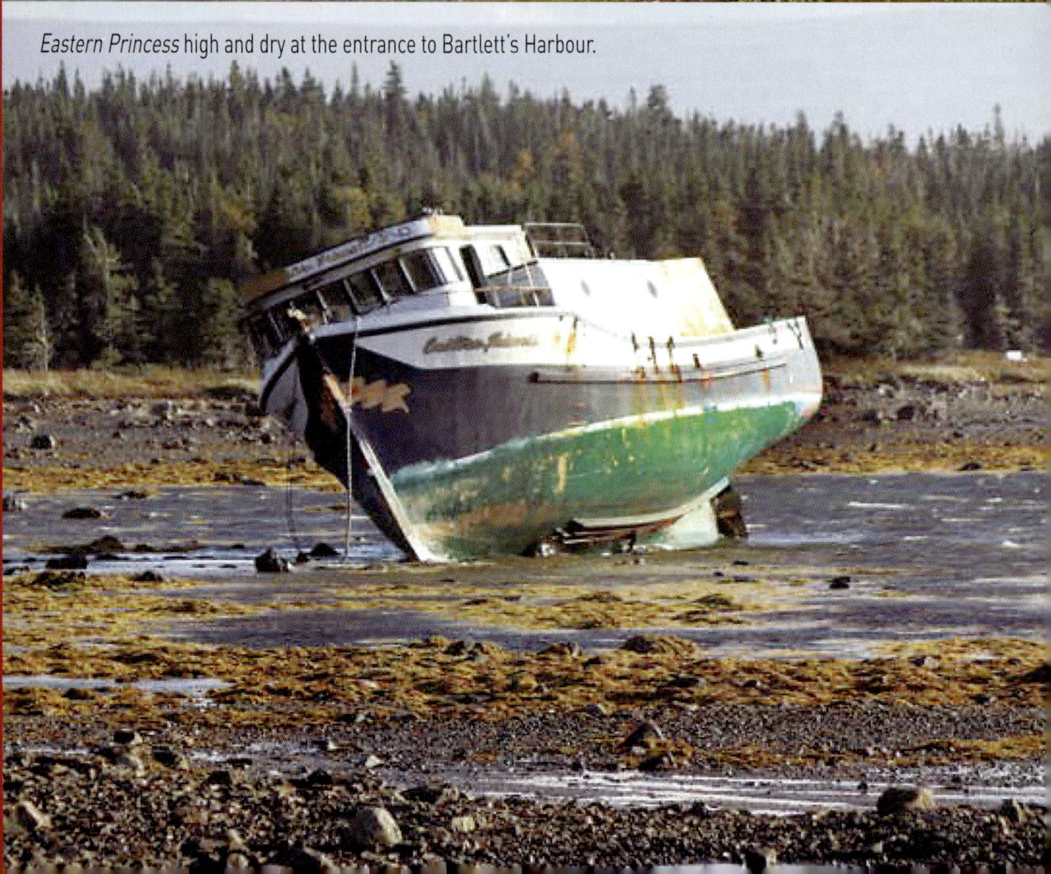
Eastern Princess high and dry at the entrance to Bartlett's Harbour.

Brig Bay's Morris Point and Darby's Island.

came to the area in the late 1700s. A lobster factory operated in Brig Bay for over 100 years. In the late 1920s, logging and fishing were the major employment sources.

A few kilometres southwest of Brig Bay is Bird Cove, settled in 1873. Cod, lobster, and herring fisheries were the primary traditional industries. Thirty-eight Aboriginal archaeology sites were discovered there in the 1990s; seven have been excavated, including one of Maritime Archaic people from 4350 BCE. An old schoolhouse was converted into the 50 Centuries Interpretation Centre, which explores the history and cultures of the area. Walking trails on nearby Dog Peninsula are ideal for birdwatchers.

Plum Point (population 100) has long relied on fishing; Basque and French fishers based their seasonal operations there. When Route 430 was completed in 1969, Plum Point became a service centre for the area. The Plum Point Motel and Restaurant is popular with visitors to the area, as well as those continuing on to L'Anse aux Meadows National Historic Site or to catch the ferry to Labrador at St. Barbe (see Trip 12).

From Plum Point, bike southwest on Route 430 to return to Eddies Cove West.

Point Amour Lighthouse.

12

Labrador Coast

Pidgeon Cove-St. Barbe, Newfoundland, to Red Bay, Labrador

> **Distance:** 257 km
>> **Primary road(s):** Trans-Labrador Highway, Route 510
>>> **Amenities:** L'Anse-au-Claire, L'Anse-au-Loup, Red Bay

If you have time to spend a day in Labrador as part of your travels up the Great Northern Peninsula, this ride is an excellent option. For a greater adventure, ride the full 1,149 kilometres of the paved Trans-Labrador Highway—all the way across the Big Land—but for this trip, we'll stick to the Labrador Coastal Drive.

This trip begins in Pidgeon Cove-St. Barbe, about 19 kilometres north of Plum Point (Trip 11), where you catch the ferry to Blanc-Sablon, Quebec, a 2-hour trip. From Blanc-Sablon, take Route 510 (the Trans-Labrador Highway) to Red Bay, Labrador, and return to overnight in L'Anse-au-Clair, also in Labrador.

Ensure that you have a ferry reservation for you and your motorcycle for the day you wish to travel, especially in the summer.

Blanc-Sablon is adjacent to the town of L'Anse-au-Clair. The paved road from L'Anse-au-Clair to Red Bay is 81 kilometres, generally along a sandy coastline dotted with small communities, and is called the Labrador Straits.

Ferry information: Labrador Marine (1-709-877-2222 in St. Barbe or 1-418-461-2889 in Blanc-Sablon). Reservations are recommended.

It is at least a 3- to 4-hour ride to Red Bay and return to L'Anse-au-Clair; it is better to allow 6 or more hours to sightsee and eat along the way. If you take a morning ferry out of St. Barbe, you will be in L'Anse-au-Clair by noon. Check into your hotel in L'Anse-au-Clair early, leaving the rest of the day to

Dara Desgagnes, a tanker from Montreal in L'Anse-au-Loup.

Old family home in Capstan Island.

travel to and from Red Bay and return in time for supper.

Take Route 510 out of L'Anse-au-Clair. Within 10 kilometres, you will be in Forteau (population 377). Forteau, which means "strong water" in English, is situated in Forteau Bay, along with the communities of English Point and Buckles Point. The International Grenfell Association built its first nursing station in Forteau in 1909; in 2024, the Labrador Straits Health Centre is a mainstay in Forteau.

The Point Amour Lighthouse in nearby L'Anse-Amour ("love cove") is a provincial historic site. A burial mound in the area dates back 7,500 years to Maritime Archaic people. Another landmark in L'Anse-Amour is the wreck of the HMS *Raleigh*, which sank in 1926. The hiking trails near L'Anse-Amour are popular with local residents and tourists.

Return to Route 510 and ride about 5 kilometres to L'Anse-au-Loup ("cove of wolves," population 500+), which

West St. Modeste.

A capstan in Red Bay.

Old vessel in Red Bay harbour.

was frequented by French, English, Scottish and Irish settlers, who fished and hunted seals. The Labrador Fishermen's Union Shrimp Company Ltd. is a significant employer in L'Anse-au-Loup. It was in L'Anse-au-Loup that I first experienced the notorious blackflies of Labrador—they were so thick that I could barely take photos—a danger of travelling in Labrador in the summer (don't forget your insect repellent!).

Eleven kilometres northeast of L'Anse-au-Loup is Capstan Island, a small community that took its name from a small island offshore. A capstan is a wooden post with a cable attached for pulling traps into boats or boats out of the water. Another small community, West St. Modeste, is located about 3 kilometres northeast of Capstan Island. Dr. Wilfred Grenfell

opened a co-op store there in 1903.

Next is Pinware River Provincial Park, situated at the mouth of the large Pinware River, one of the province's most storied salmon rivers.

Our destination on Route 510 is Red Bay, known worldwide for its underwater sites. From the 1500s up to the 1700s, it was home to a major Basque whaling station. Some of the whaling boats sank offshore; 1,000 barrels of whale oil were discovered aboard a sunken vessel off Red Bay when the area was explored between 1978 and 1985. Red Bay was designated a UNESCO World Heritage Site in 2013; a community museum offers a detailed history of this fascinating area.

Return to L'Anse-au-Clair by riding south on Route 510.

Boat in St. Lunaire-Griquet.

⑬ Road to L'Anse aux Meadows National Historic Site

Anchor Point to L'Anse aux Meadows

> **Distance:** 270 km
>> **Primary road(s):** Routes 430, 436
>>> **Amenities:** Anchor Point, Flowers Cove, St. Lunaire-Griquet

Trip 13 is a ride across the northern tip of the Great Northern Peninsula from Anchor Point to L'Anse aux Meadows National Historic Site and back.

Anchor Point (population 300), settled by English sailor Robert Bartlett, was the first English settlement on the French coast. Traditional industries included salmon fishing, seal harvesting, and farming.

From Anchor Point, ride 9 kilometres northeast on Route 430 to Flowers Cove. Tourists visit Flowers Cove to see trombolites, fossils made from bacteria and algae that date to 650 million years ago. Flowers Cove and Western Australia are the two places in the world where trombolites are prolific.

Five kilometres beyond Flowers Cove on Route 430 take the left exit into Savage Cove, the northernmost sheltered harbour on the Strait of Belle Isle. Twenty-one kilometres northeast of Savage Cove is the fishing and logging community of Eddies Cove, also known as Eddies Cove East to differentiate it from Eddies Cove West (Trip 11).

While in Eddies Cove (East), I stopped to take some photos but I was fascinated by a small river running under a highway bridge. I was intrigued by the rocks that had created small waterfalls (see photo page 84).

From Eddies Cove, ride east 67 kilometres across the Great Northern Peninsula on Route 430 toward St. Anthony. Instead of turning south at the Viking Lodge Motel in Pistolet

Seal skins stretched and drying, Savage Cove.
Eddies Cove.

Barbe Bay and Anchor Point.

Bay and heading south to St. Anthony, turn left onto Route 436 and ride northeast on it toward the Viking settlement in L'Anse aux Meadows.

St. Lunaire-Griquet (population 600) is about 17 kilometres northeast along Route 436. Its primary industries are fishing and tourism. One notable business venture is the Dark Tickle Company Economusée in St. Lunaire, famous for its jams and sauces, which can be purchased provincewide. The économusée features a well-travelled interpretative walk along a boardwalk to wild berry grounds.

About 7 more kilometres along Route 436 a right turn onto Quirpon Road leads to Quirpon. Just offshore is Quirpon Island; a local company, Linkum Tours, offers 10 fully restored rooms in Quirpon Lighthouse, food, and boating tours to view whales and icebergs.

Backtrack on Quirpon Road and turn right on Route 436. In 6 kilometres, you'll reach L'Anse aux Meadows National

Sod structure.

No hour is wasted
when spent on two wheels.

—Anonymous

L'Anse aux Meadows.

Historic Site of Canada, which became a UNESCO World Heritage Site in 1978. This site is well worth the 434-kilometre ride from the TCH in Deer Lake.

The L'Anse aux Meadows National Historic Site, settled over 1,000 years ago by the Norse or Vikings, measures about 30 square miles and, in this area, over 2,000 Viking artifacts have been found. The site has eight buildings constructed using sod over wooden frames. L'Anse aux Meadows is the only confirmed Viking site in or close to North America.

The archaeologists who worked at L'Anse aux Meadows say that the buildings on site were living quarters and workshops that the Vikings constructed. The site is well marked and explained. Take a guided tour or speak to Viking-garbed workers. Plan on spending at least 2 to 3 hours at this site to enjoy the whole experience.

Leaving Anchor Point in the early morning and returning via The Viking Trail in late afternoon is another spectacular day on the Rock.

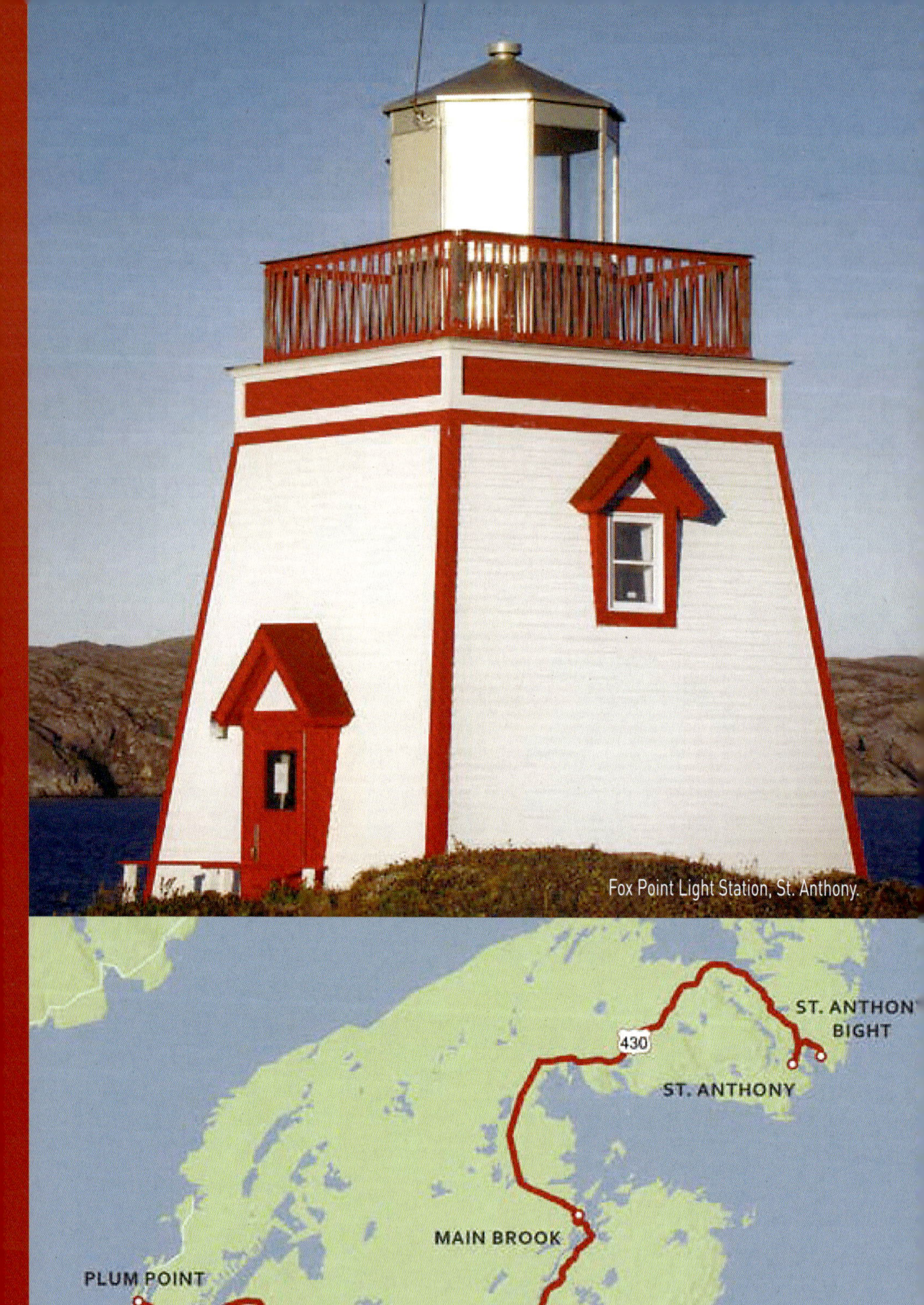

Fox Point Light Station, St. Anthony.

14 Top of Great Northern Peninsula

St. Anthony Bight to Plum Point

> **Distance:** 342 km
>> **Primary road(s):** Routes 430, 432
>>> **Amenities:** St. Anthony

This trip takes you from St. Anthony Bight to Plum Point and back.

Formerly known as St. Mein Bay, St. Anthony Bight was settled by the French. Icebergs travelling by Newfoundland through "Iceberg Alley" are often grounded in the inlets around St. Anthony Bight, even as late as August.

Throughout this trip, you'll see roadside vegetable gardens. Over generations, people have learned which plants thrive in the area's short growing seasons and cold temperatures. On the Great Northern Peninsula, most homes face a stark, barren, rocky coastline.

But in the late 1960s, as the Newfoundland government began to push roads through to these isolated communities, topsoil was churned up, much of it fertile. Soon residents began planting food crops in this soil, fencing their plots with old lumber and wire to keep moose, caribou, and other wildlife out and erecting scarecrows to deter birds and other scavengers. As the roads are well maintained and the traffic is low, it is a biker's paradise.

From St. Anthony Bight, visit St. Anthony (population 2,200) at the northeast part of Route 430. With summer festivals and other attractions, St. Anthony is one of the main towns on the peninsula, offering many options for accommodations and restaurants. To enjoy marine life, take a boat tour such as the Northland Discovery Boat Tours: you

may see icebergs, whales, dolphins, and bird-nesting colonies.

In 1900, the English doctor Wilfred Grenfell came to this area. He set up a Grenfell Mission in Red Bay, Labrador, but later focused on St. Anthony for his medical practice. The Grenfell Historic Properties include the Grenfell Interpretation Centre, the Grenfell House Museum, and Grenfell Handicrafts Store. Grenfell and his wife, Lady Anne, are buried at Tea House Hill in St. Anthony. The Grenfell name is visible all over the northern part of the Great Northern Peninsula and southern Labrador.

From St. Anthony, head west along Route 430. About 52 kilometres from St. Anthony, turn left onto Route 432 and ride south toward Main Brook. From Main Brook, stay on Route 432 going in a westerly direction to Plum Point.

Main Brook is on the southwest shore of Hare Bay where the Maritime Archaic people lived before the French and English settlers arrived. In the 1940s, the Bowater Paper Company started operations and Main Brook flourished as a forestry company town. Later, fishing and tourism would become important industries. The Tuckamore Lodge and Outfitters is a popular place in Main Brook.

As you leave Main Brook, bike westward 87 kilometres on Route 432 to Plum Point. Most of this stretch is through peaceful wilderness country.

At Plum Point, a signpost behind the Plum Point Motel and Restaurant gives a brief history of Captain James Cook and his visits to this part of the Great Northern Peninsula.

This return trip across the top of the Great Northern Peninsula can easily take a full day if you want to stop for food, sightseeing, and photos.

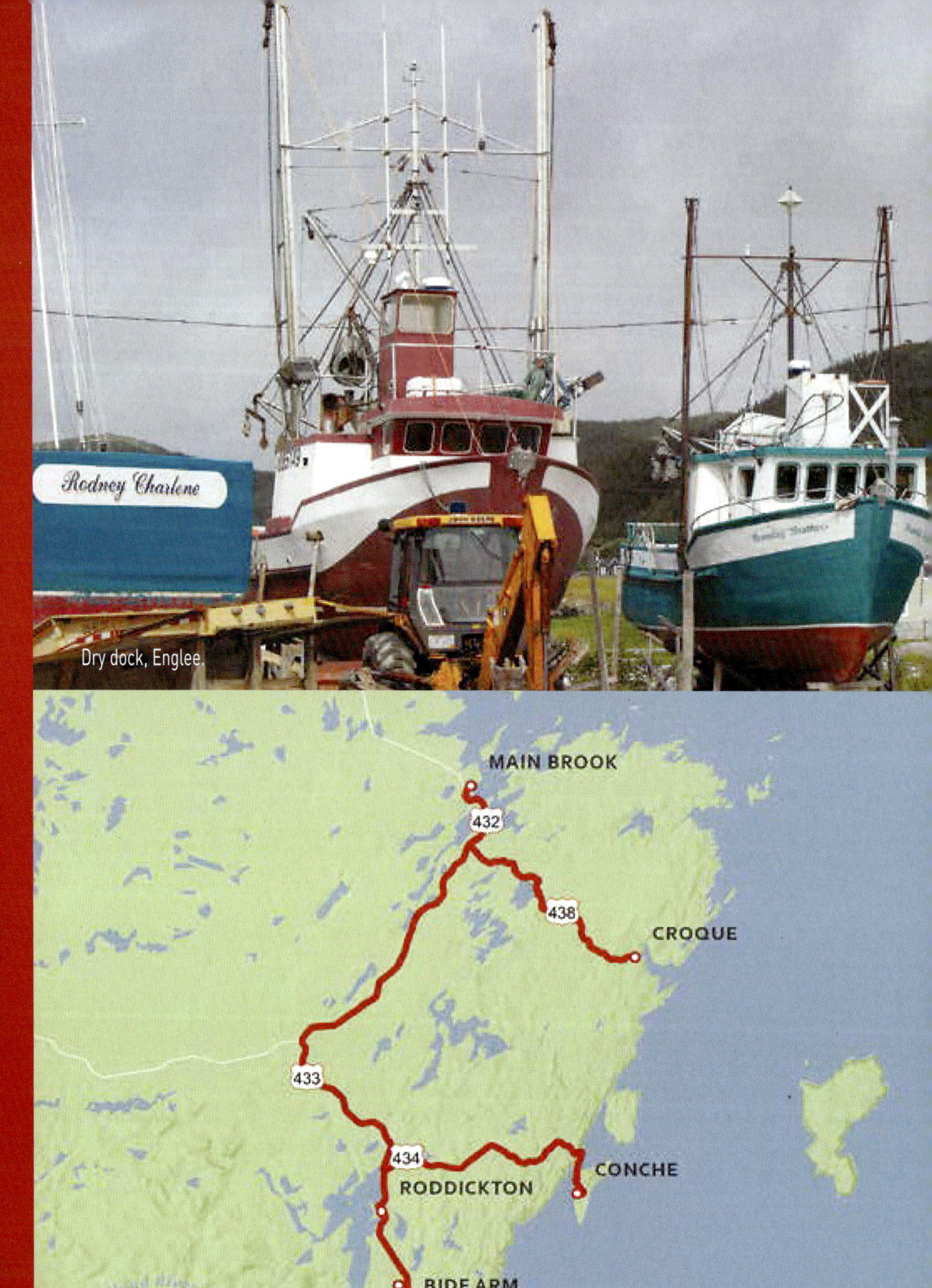

Rodney Charlene
Dry dock, Englee.
MAIN BROOK
432
438
CROQUE
433
434
RODDICKTON
CONCHE
BIDE ARM
ENGLEE

Northeast Side of Great Northern Peninsula

Main Brook to Englee

> **Distance:** 218 km
>> **Primary road(s):** Routes 432, 433, 434, 438
>>> **Amenities:** Roddickton–Bide Arm, Englee

This route south of L'Anse aux Meadows National Historic Site is not well travelled, but it is spectacular. Trip 15 takes you along the eastern side of the Great Northern Peninsula, with side trips to Croque and Conche en route to Englee.

From Main Brook, head south on Route 432 (Main Brook Highway). After 7 kilometres, turn left onto Route 438 (Croque Road). From this exit awaits 20 kilometres of winding, gravel road to Croque. If you are riding an off-road motorcycle, this presents no problem; otherwise, you have to consider if you want to take the road—you may have to ride slowly to avoid the potholes—and the chance of damaging your bike.

Croque (population 45), boasts a traditional fishing store waterfront. From Croque, continue on to the even smaller community of Grandois-St. Juliens. The Epine Cadoret Trail along the way leads to the mouth of Croque harbour, exhibiting carvings from French sailors made in mid-1800s.

Return to Route 432 and ride 23 kilometres south to the exit onto Route 433 (Englee Road). Ride south on Route 433 for 15 kilometres, then exit onto the paved Route 434 (Conche Road).

Conche (population 150) was visited by French explorers as early as 1613. This area of Newfoundland— the eastern side of the Great

Garbage box, Roddickton.

Row of rubber boots on
a fish-drying platform, Conche.

Bide Arm.

Northern Peninsula around to the Baie Verte Peninsula—was long recognized as the French Shore. By the mid-1800s, permanent settlers from Ireland had arrived. In 2024, Conche is a beautiful, quiet community.

Ride back on Route 434 and exit south onto Route 433 to Roddickton-Bide Arm. These amalgamated communities have a combined population of about 900, most of whom live in Roddickton. Sawmills were a main source of income for people in this region in the early 1900s.

Continue south on Route 433 for 10 kilometres to the end of the road in Englee (population 489) in a sheltered harbour on the northern headland of Canada Bay.

French fishers, trappers, and builders arrived in Englee in the mid- to late 1800s. By 1940, Canada Bay Cold Storage had built a fresh-frozen cod and salmon operation there. A marine centre in Englee, Sealand Enterprise Ltd., specializes in boat building and modifications.

Return to Main Brook on Routes 433 and 423. This trip is 218 kilometres if you travel in and out of Croque and Conche on the way down.

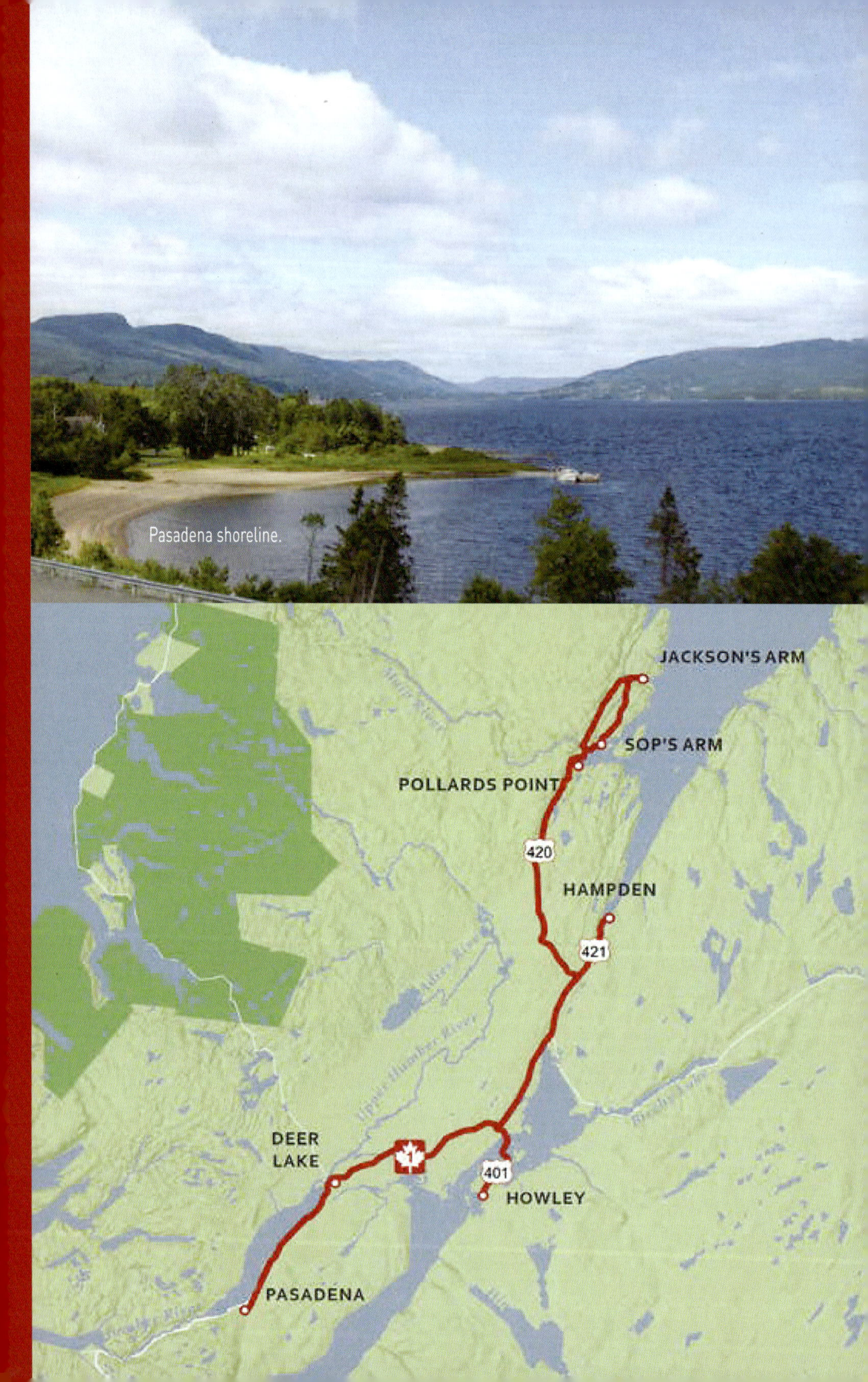

Pasadena shoreline.

JACKSON'S ARM
SOP'S ARM
POLLARDS POINT
420
HAMPDEN
421
DEER LAKE
401
HOWLEY
PASADENA

Southeast Side of Great Northern Peninsula

Pasadena to Jackson's Arm

> **Distance:** 328 km
>> **Primary road(s):** TCH; Routes 401, 420, 421
>>> **Amenities:** Howley, Pasadena, Deer Lake

This trip may seem short when viewed on a map, but the return trip covers about 328 kilometres and many of the roads north of the TCH are paved but winding and require reduced speed.

The town of Pasadena (population 3,524) was a traditional farming area but the population grew during the 1950s and 1960s. By 1986, Pasadena amalgamated with the nearby communities of Midland and South Brook and the new town upgraded to better water and sewage facilities and improved streets. Many young families moved from other west coast communities to become a part of the new town and enjoy its beaches, parks, ball fields, playgrounds, hiking, and cross-country skiing. Pasadena is also close to Marble Mountain Resort and its downhill-skiing runs. Pasadena Beach Park's beautiful sandy beaches are popular with swimmers, boaters, and jet skiers.

From Pasadena, ride 25 kilometres northeast on the TCH along the edge of Deer Lake to the town of Deer Lake. Along this stretch you'll pass the communities of Pynn's Brook and St. Judes as well as a hydroelectric plant on the Humber River. The TCH in this area is well maintained and wide, split into separate east- and westbound lanes.

Continue about 29 kilometres east past Deer Lake to a right-hand exit into Howley. This road passes ponds, lakes, cabins, and summer homes.

Howley (population 179) has a pub, a convenience store, a B&B, a campground, a hotel, and other amenities. A park, created

Howley war memorial.

in 2004, is dedicated to the four moose that were introduced to the island of Newfoundland from New Brunswick in 1904 as a food source. Now over 100,000 of these majestic creatures roam the province's woods, backyards, and highways—a biker must always watch for moose. The residents of Howley created this small park with a moose statue to celebrate 100 years of moose residency.

Backtrack 14 kilometres to the TCH and ride northeast to the exit to Route 420. Route 420 north from the TCH is a winding road—but it is paved and the riding is enjoyable, if at a relatively slow pace. Be mindful of your gas gauge as the road is long with only a few gas stations.

Pollards Point, the first town you encounter, does have a gas station. Seven kilometres north of Pollards Point is Sop's Arm (population 157), known for its salmon fishing and white-water kayaking. An island just offshore, called Sop's Island, was resettled in the mid-1950s and now has many cabins.

Another 16 kilometres north of Sop's Arm is Jackson's Arm, a community settled by John Wicks of Christchurch, England, around 1870. A ferry once ran from Jackson's Arm to Great Harbour Deep, 78 kilometres north. Great Harbour Deep was resettled in 2002 and the ferry became obsolete.

The Deer Lake power plant.

SAPP Recreation Centre.

White Bay from a Hampden wharf.

Moose memorial in Howley.

Travel back Route 420 for about 56 kilometres and turn left at the Hampden exit on Route 421. Ride 11 kilometres to Hampden and then cruise along the shoreline for 4 kilometres to the Beaches in White Bay. One of two islands in the bay next to Hampden is Millers Island, where a tuberculosis graveyard from 1924 is located.

Leave Hampden and return to Pasadena to complete this 328-kilometre day trip.

Fishing sheds, Seal Cove.

FLEUR DE LYS
COACHMAN'S COVE
410
WILD COVE
BAIE VERTE
419
SEAL COVE
412
411
WESTPORT

17 Baie Verte Peninsula West

> Distance: **201 km**
>> Primary road(s): **Routes 410, 411, 412, 419**
>>> Amenities: **Baie Verte**

Once you leave the TCH at Sheppardville and head north onto the Baie Verte Peninsula, you are travelling on Route 410 (the Dorset Trail). This 90-kilometre highway runs south to north from the TCH up through the peninsula. Much of this trip is side trips off the main Route 410.

The Dorset Trail is named after the Dorset people who lived here 15 centuries ago. Before them, the Maritime Archaic people were in the area; much later, European settlers arrived.

Because of the geography and number of communities on the Baie Verte Peninsula, I have broken it into two rides— this one travels the western side. If you are going to be on the Baie Verte Peninsula for a night or two, you can camp in Flatwater Pond Park or book a hotel in Baie Verte.

This trip starts in Westport (population 185), the first permanent settlement on the Baie Verte Peninsula, and continues on paved roads to Seal Cove, Wild Cove, Baie Verte, Coachman's Cove, and Fleur de Lys.

From Westport, ride 27 kilometres to Route 410 and continue north on Route 410 for about 15 kilometres to the town of Baie Verte. Take the left-hand exit to Route 412 (Seal Cove Road), near the Baie Vista Inn. Ride toward the coastal communities of Seal Cove and Wild Cove on the western side of the peninsula. After a look around Seal Cove (population 281), continue along Route 412 to a left-hand turn into the

Coachman's Cove.

Precariously perched
on Fleur de Lys harbour.

small community of Wild Cove (population 50) on Route 419.

Backtrack along Routes 419 and 412 to Baie Verte. The town boomed in the mid-1950s when asbestos, copper, lead, zinc, and gold were mined. Baie Verte's amenities include a tourist information centre, the Dorset Craft Shop, and the Miner's Museum, which is built over an abandoned copper mine.

Advocate Mining Co. operated an open pit mine in the Baie Verte area in 1955. Although there is still plenty of asbestos, the mine shut down in 1981 due to an awareness of the health hazards of asbestos.

From Baie Verte, ride north along Route 410 for about 17 kilometres before exiting right into Coachman's Cove (population 111). Coachman's Cove was once called *Pot d'Etain*, French for Tiny Pot Islands. French fishers have been in the area since the early 19th century; later, English and Irish fishers also came to the area, pursuing cod and herring. By 1935, lumber and sawmill ventures were operational in the area. In 1999/2000, a Paleo-Eskimo site was discovered, dating back 3,000 years and indicating even older origins in this community.

No one weaves the exquisite quite like Mother Nature.

—Foster Kinn, *Freedom's Rush: Tales from the Biker and the Beast*

Fleur de Lys.

Head back to Route 410, and ride 9 kilometres to Fleur de Lys (population 207), the most northerly community on that highway. The fleur de lys has always been a symbol used by French royalty to represent its Catholic saints. Fleur de Lys is a great place to see icebergs, whales, and seabirds entering provincial waters along Iceberg Alley. Four trails—Spotted Point Trail, Hummocks Trail, Ocean View Trail, and Fleur de Lys Lookout—offer views of the ocean and, in season, icebergs.

This sheltered harbour has been used for 45 centuries. Originally, Maritime Archaic people settled here. And, 15 centuries afterwards, the Groswater Paleo-Eskimo people arrived. And, another half a century later, the Middle Dorset people came; they used the area's soft soapstone to make cooking pots. The soapstone quarry here received national historic site status in 1966. You can learn about these quarries in the interpretation centre next to the quarry.

The direct return trip from Fleur de Lys to Westport is 72 kilometres.

Shelley's Island, Fleur de Lys.

Cod drying, Fleur de Lys.

Burlington.

PACQUET
MING'S BIGHT
LASCIE
417
BRENT'S COVE
WOODSTOCK
HARBOUR
418
ROUND
414
SHOE COVE
410
413
BURLINGTON
MIDDLE ARM

⑱ Baie Verte Peninsula East

> **Distance:** 251 km
>> **Primary road(s):** Routes 410, 413, 414, 417, 418
>>> **Amenities:** Burlington, LaScie

When you leave the TCH near Sheppardville and head north onto the Baie Verte Peninsula, you'll be travelling on Route 410, or the Dorset Trail, named for Dorset Eskimos who lived in the area 1,500 years ago. This 90-kilometre highway runs south to north from the TCH through the peninsula. Some communities lie along the Dorset Trail, including Fleur de Lys at the northerly tip; others, west and east off it.

Because the Baie Verte Peninsula encompasses such a large area, it deserves to be broken into two separate trips—this one travels the western side. If you are going to be on the peninsula overnight, camp in Flatwater Pond Park or book accommodations in the town of Baie Verte.

This trip starts in Burlington and continues north and then east to Ming's Bight, Woodstock, Pacquet, Harbour Round, Brent's Cove, Shoe Cove, and LaScie. Including all the side trips, this route is 163 kilometres (all paved roads) from Burlington to LaScie, plus 88 kilometres straight back to the start. To get to Burlington, turn onto Route 413 from the Dorset Trail and ride 23 kilometres.

Burlington is the home of singer Rex Goudie and comedian Shaun Majumdar. This small community (population 304 in 2021) is also home to The Gathering, a summer food and music festival. Known for its fishing and forestry, Burlington was originally named Northwest Arm.

Route 413 continues 8 kilometres southwest to the

community of Middle Arm, for an additional side trip. To leave Burlington, backtrack 23 kilometres on Route 413 and exit right onto the Dorset Trail. Ride 12 kilometres and then exit right onto Route 414.

Ride 12 kilometres on Route 414, then turn left onto Route 418 and ride to Ming's Bight (population 298), located between White Bay and Notre Dame Bay, a community wrapped around its bay like a horseshoe.

Leaving Ming's Bight, travel south on Route 418 and back to Route 414. Turn left and ride 10 kilometres to the exit to Route 417 toward Woodstock and Pacquet. Woodstock (population 195) is a fishing community at the head of Northwest Arm. At the entrance to Woodstock is a shed with a boat painted on it, the first of a collection of photograph-worthy sheds. Continue north for another 4 kilometres on Route 417 to Pacquet (population 145), a French name that translates *hideaway* in English. As with others on this coast, it was historically a fishing and lumbering community. French fishers visited this area as far back as 1713.

A gazebo and picnic area in Pacquet offer a view over Northwest Arm and Pacquet Harbour. The eating area is adjacent to the municipal hall, fire department, post office,

Fishing gear, Middle Arm.

Shoe Cove building on stilts.

and a Veterans Memorial Park, which honours the 26 residents from Pacquet and Woodstock who lost their lives in World Wars I and II and the Korean War.

Backtrack on Route 417 to Route 414; turn left and ride east for 19 kilometres to the exit into Harbour Round and Brent's Cove. The exit is about 19 kilometres away on Route 414. As you travel north into Harbour Round (population 188) and Brent's Cove (population 119), look for the old lumber mill on the roadside as you ride toward Harbour Round. Next along Route 414 is a right-hand exit to Shoe Cove. Ride along Shoe Cove Road to the marina, where you may see residents drying their catch, in season and when weather conditions are optimal.

LaScie (population 820) is about 7 kilometres northwest of Shoe Cove. Historically, Europeans, including the Basque and the French, fished and settled in LaScie. The harbour, with its public wharf and many private wharves, is generally busy. Visit Outport Museum to learn more about the history of the area; the attached tea room serves Newfoundland main courses and desserts.

From LaScie, return to Burlington to complete the trip.

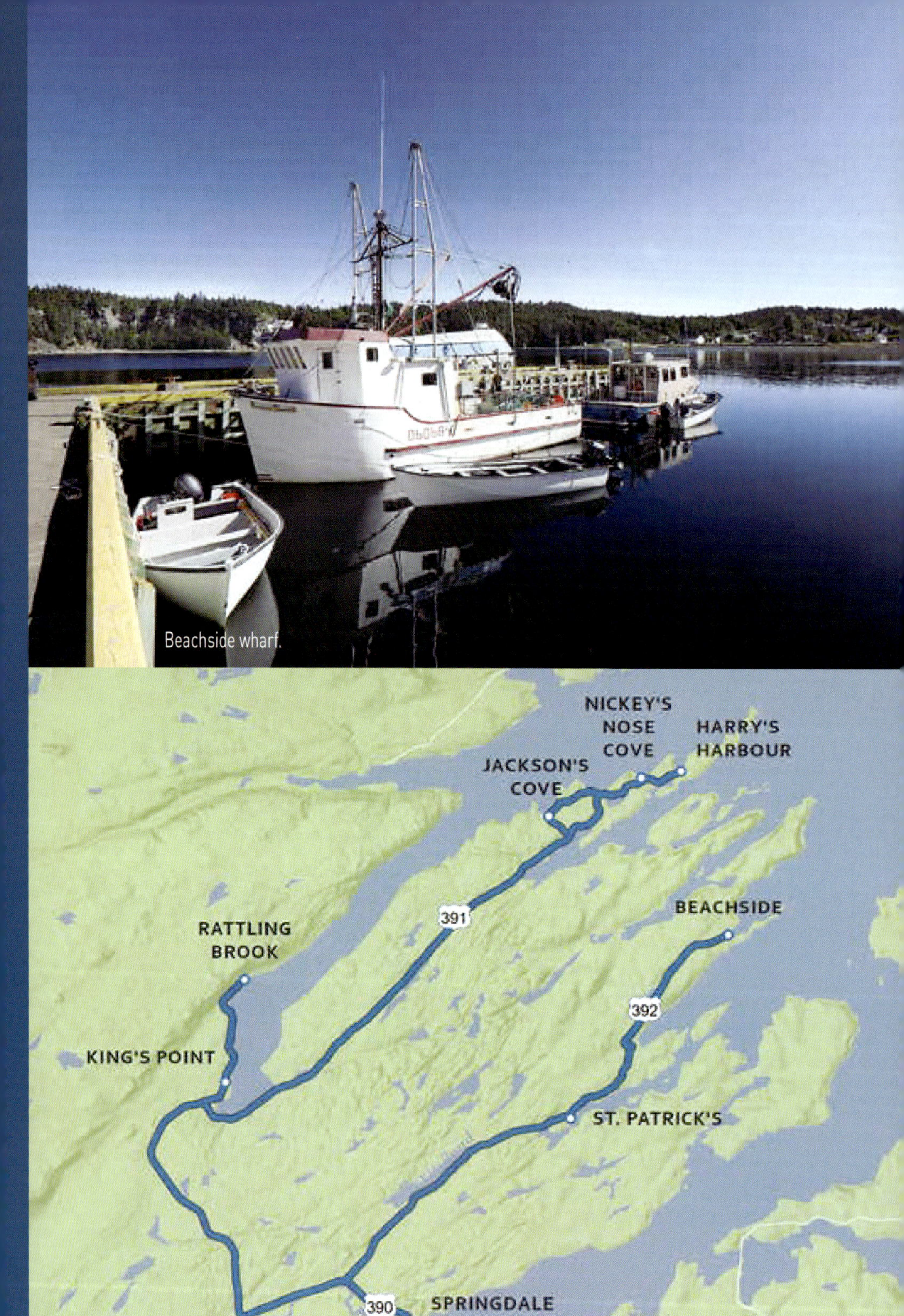
Beachside wharf.
NICKEY'S
NOSE
COVE
HARRY'S
HARBOUR
JACKSON'S
COVE
391
BEACHSIDE
RATTLING
BROOK
392
KING'S POINT
ST. PATRICK'S
390
SPRINGDALE

19 Springdale Exit

> Distance: **153 km**
>> Primary road(s): **Routes 390, 391, 392**
>>> Amenities: **Springdale, King's Point**

This day trip from Springdale (population 2,965), the largest town on the peninsula, is a 153-kilometre ride. Springdale, with its regional hospital, sports facilities, government agencies, and amenities, is considered the hub of Green Bay.

The Springdale area has been the home of many Indigenous people, including Beothuk, Mi'kmaq, Dorset, and Maritime Archaic people. Springdale is situated in Halls Bay, named for a Captain Hall from King's County, Nova Scotia, who arrived in the mid-18th century when the Beothuk were the area's main inhabitants.

By the late 1800s, European settlers had started a sawmilling operation near Springdale. Mainmast Museum, H.C. Grant Heritage Museum, and the Springdale Heritage Society, all in Springdale, tell the area's history and house artifacts from Halls Bay.

Leave Springdale and return to the intersection with Route 390. Turn right onto Route 392 and ride northeast to St. Patricks (population 50).

After St. Patricks, continue for 11 kilometres on Route 392 to Beachside (population 97). This picturesque community, located on the north side of Little Bay, was known as Wild Bight in the 19th century. From Beachside, you may ride west toward the community of Southern Arm, 2 kilometres away.

Travel back Route 392, bypass the exit into Springdale, continue on to Route 390, and turn right onto Route 391,

King's Point.

Harry's Harbour cove.

Jackson's Cove.

Springdale.

heading northwest toward King's Point. From Beachside to the beginning of Route 391 is 27 kilometres.

King's Point (population 653), with restaurants, accommodations, and King's Point Pottery, is a popular tourist stop. Watch for whales, seals, and eagles along the coast. Hike the 8-kilometre Alexander Murray Hiking Trail, which leads to a panoramic viewpoint. While in King's Point, head northward along Main Street for 6 kilometres to Rattling Brook, with its series of waterfalls.

From King's Point, reconnect with Route 391 and ride northeast 21 kilometres to the left-hand exit into Jackson's Cove, where you'll find the Ocean View Walking Trail. From Jackson's Cove, ride northeast along the coast through Langdon Cove to Nickey's Nose Cove, 5 kilometres away.

Back on Route 391, ride 2 kilometres to Harry's Harbour, which has accommodations as well as walking trails. Return to Springdale via Routes 391 and 390.

Mussel farming off the causeway to Sunday Cove Island.

South Brook Exit plus Ferries

> **Distance:** 172 km
>> **Primary road(s):** Routes 380, 381, 382
>>> **Amenities:** South Brook, Triton, Pilley's Island, Robert's Arm

This Central Newfoundland trip would take about 3.5 hours if you simply rode from South Brook and followed the three-prong route suggested here. I recommend taking the day and enjoying the scenery, the pit stops, the food, and conversations with residents.

South Brook (population 420) is named for the salmon river that passes through the community and into Halls Bay to the north. That river runs from South Pond, which is south of town near Kona Beach Park. The South Brook Hiking Trail, Goodyear's Cove Park, and ATV trails are located in this area.

Leaving South Brook, ride 20 kilometres down Route 380 to the exit to Route 381 (Port Anson Road). Turn left toward Port Anson and Miles Cove. Both communities are on Sunday Cove Island, accessible by a causeway. Large mussel farming operations are visible on the approach to Sunday Cove Island. Continue across the causeway and eastward to Port Anson (population 42) on Notre Dame Bay. Miles Cove (population 97) is 6 kilometres farther down the road.

Backtrack 15 kilometres on Route 381 and turn left onto Route 380. Ride 5 kilometres to Robert's Arm (population 722), Green Bay. Fishing, lumber, mining, and pulpwood were the primary industries of Robert's Arm over the centuries; Bowaters Pulp and Paper Company was the main employer through the 20th century. Today, Robert's Arm is a quiet retirement community. Because of the abundance of

Triton.

snowshoe hare, the community was called Rabbits Arm until the early 1900s. Robert's Arm is located near Crescent Lake, which is rumoured to have its own lake monster, Cressie.

From Robert's Arm, ride 9 kilometres east on Route 380 toward Pilley's Island. Instead of going into Pilley's Island, turn left onto Route 382 north to the ferry to Long Island (see schedule for the Long Island-Pilley's Island Ferry at 511nl.ca or https://www.gov.nl.ca/ti/ferryservices/schedules/). You can take your bike across on this ferry. On Long Island, you can ride 9 kilometres through the communities of Lushes

Triton fishing boat.

Bight, Beaumont, and Beaumont North. Stop at the Long Island Heritage Centre museum and café in Lushes Bight.

Until 2019, this ferry continued on to Little Bay Islands, which is still a great place to explore on foot if you can find a boat to take you there. You'd have to leave your bike parked on Long Island.

On your return from Long Island, ride back down Route 382 for 9 kilometres and turn left on Route 380 and into the community of Pilley's Island (population 286). A pyrite mine was established in Bumblebee Bight on Pilley's Island

in 1887. The Bumblebee Bight Inn and Brewery offers food and drinks.

Route 380 leads across the causeway onto Pilley's Island and, continuing eastward, across a second causeway off Pilley's Island and onto Triton Island. Triton (population 896) is a vibrant community with an abundance of sports facilities and businesses. The Triton Sperm Whale Pavilion is a tourist draw, as are whale- and iceberg-watching opportunities. The Triton Caplin Cod Festival is held each August.

Continuing north on Route 380 brings you to Brighton (population 163) on Cobbler Island, which boasts a breathtaking lookout. Look for Cobbler's Trail Lookout just as you cross the bridge into the community.

After a stop in Brighton, return to Route 380 and ride 52 kilometres back to South Brook at the TCH.

My bike beside Cressie, Robert's Arm.

Pilley's Island.

ASARCO fire truck.

21 Central Newfoundland

Buchans to Bishop's Falls

> Distance: **237 km**
>> Primary road(s): **TCH; Route 370**
>>> Amenities: **Buchans, Badger, GFW, Bishop's Falls**

This trip takes you through a part of Newfoundland that is closely tied to mining, farming, logging, power generation, and paper making.

Start in Buchans (population 590) on the northwest shore of Red Indian Lake. In the early 1900s, a prospector discovered zinc, lead, and copper ore near Buchans River and, by 1916, American Smelting and Refining Company (ASARCO) showed interest in mining the ore, marking the start of a mining industry that continues today. The original Buchans mine site is still visible; in the town, mining relics, including a company crane and an ore railway car, offer insight into the glory days of ASARCO mining. Buchans Miners Museum preserves even more of this history.

Depart Buchans and ride northeast toward Badger, beside Red Indian Lake and then Exploits River on a two-lane paved highway (Route 370). As you are riding through the forested interior, be alert for wildlife that you may encounter on this road, including moose, caribou, bear, and fox.

About 30 kilometres along Route 370 is Buchans Junction. Turn right here for a side trip to picturesque Millertown (7 kilometres each way). Return to Buchans Junction and continue toward Badger.

Badger (population 682), once famous for its large spring log drives to supply the paper mill in Grand Falls-Windsor, is named for Badger Brook, which flows through the town and is a

tributary of the Exploits River, one of the best salmon rivers in Newfoundland. ATV, hiking, and snowmobile trails run through the Badger area, as does the Trans Canada Trail. The railway ties on the town's old train trestle have been replaced by a boardwalk.

Next, head east on the TCH, travelling the banks of the Exploits River toward Grand Falls-Windsor (population 13,853). Before reaching Grand Falls-Windsor is the 18-hole Grand Falls Golf Club on the right. If you ride toward the Exploits River in Grand Falls-Windsor, you'll see the footings of the Anglo Newfoundland Development (AND) Company paper mill. One of the few remaining buildings from the mill has become the GFW Heritage Centre. Ride behind the mill site and across the bridge for a clear view of the mighty

Train trestle, Bishop's Falls.

This caribou crossed Buchans Highway in front of my bike.

Looking up the Exploits River toward the former AND Company mill site in Grand Falls-Windsor.

Exploits River. Ride a little farther up the old logging road to the Salmonid Interpretation Centre—in season, this offers a view of salmon migrating upstream.

About 4 kilometres east of the paper mill site is the Gorge Park Boat Launch & Walking Trail.

Return to the TCH and head northeast for 16 kilometres to Bishop's Falls (population 3,082). Historically, logs that escaped the AND Company mill in Grand Falls were retrieved in Bishop's Falls and returned to the mill by truck. The cross-Newfoundland train (the "Newfie Bullet") used Bishop's Falls as a central hub for many years. The 300-metre-long train trestle there—built in 1901 and the longest in Newfoundland—is now part of the Newfoundland Trailway system, used primarily by ATVs, mountain bikes, and snowmobiles.

From Fallsview Park in Bishop's Falls, the dam and power plant on the Exploits River are visible. One hundred years ago, the facilities provided electricity for the Grand Falls mill upstream and the shipping operations downstream in Botwood. In 2024, it provides electricity to the Newfoundland Power grid.

Finish this trip by riding the 117 kilometres from Bishop's Falls back to Buchans.

A bike on the road is worth two in the shed.

—Anonymous

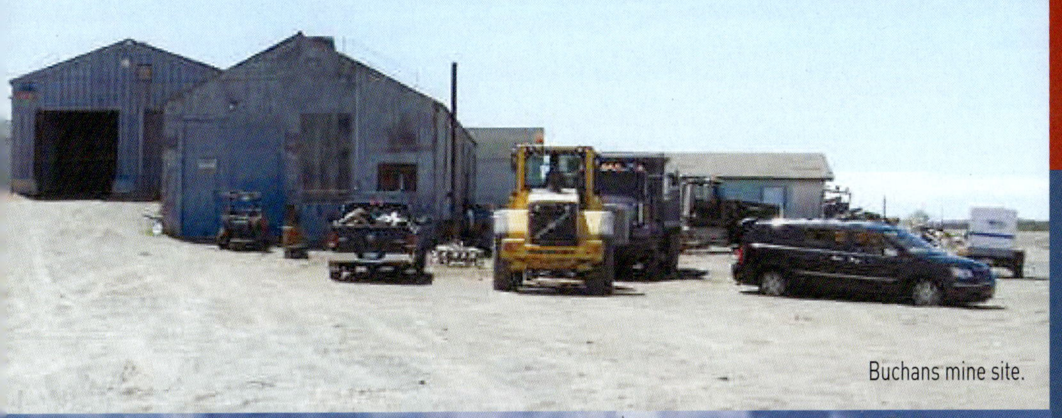

Buchans mine site.

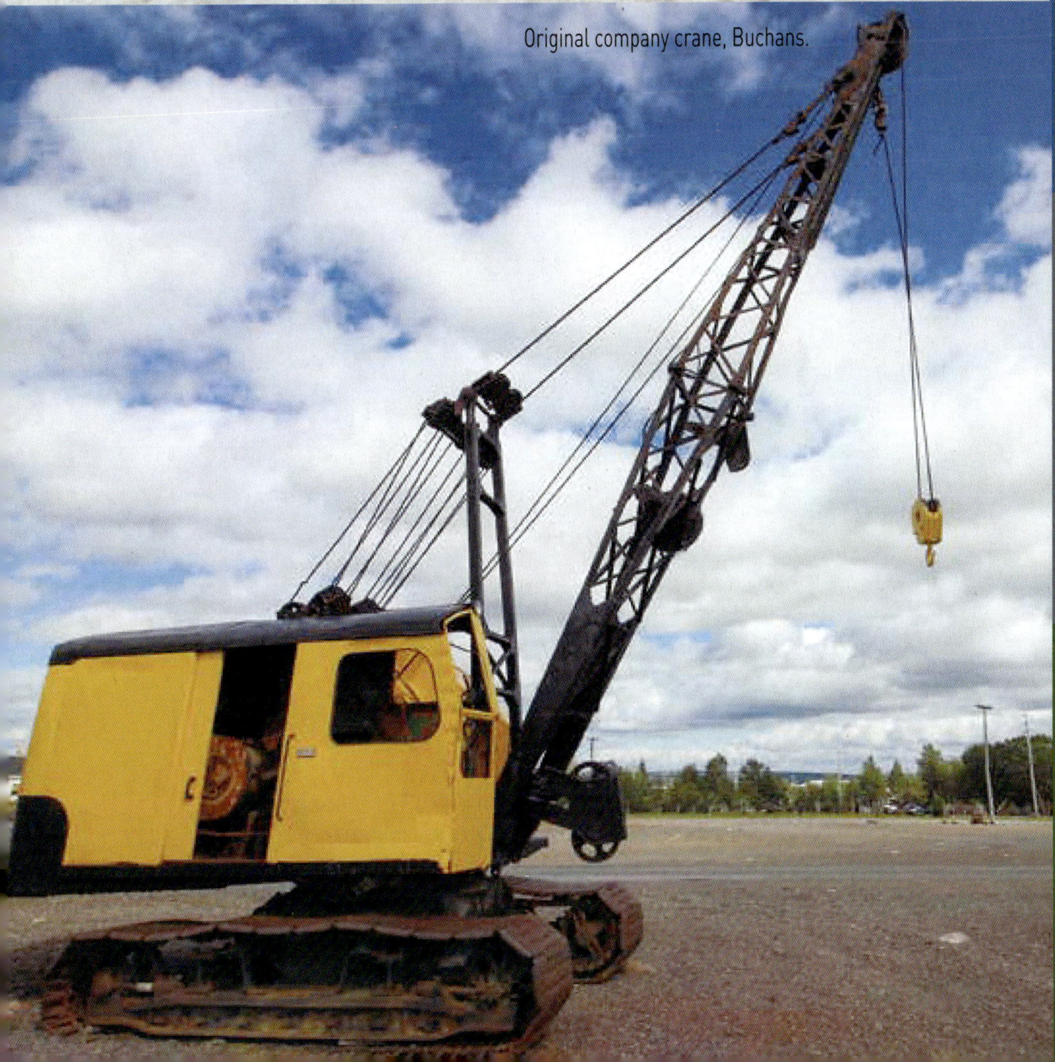

Original company crane, Buchans.

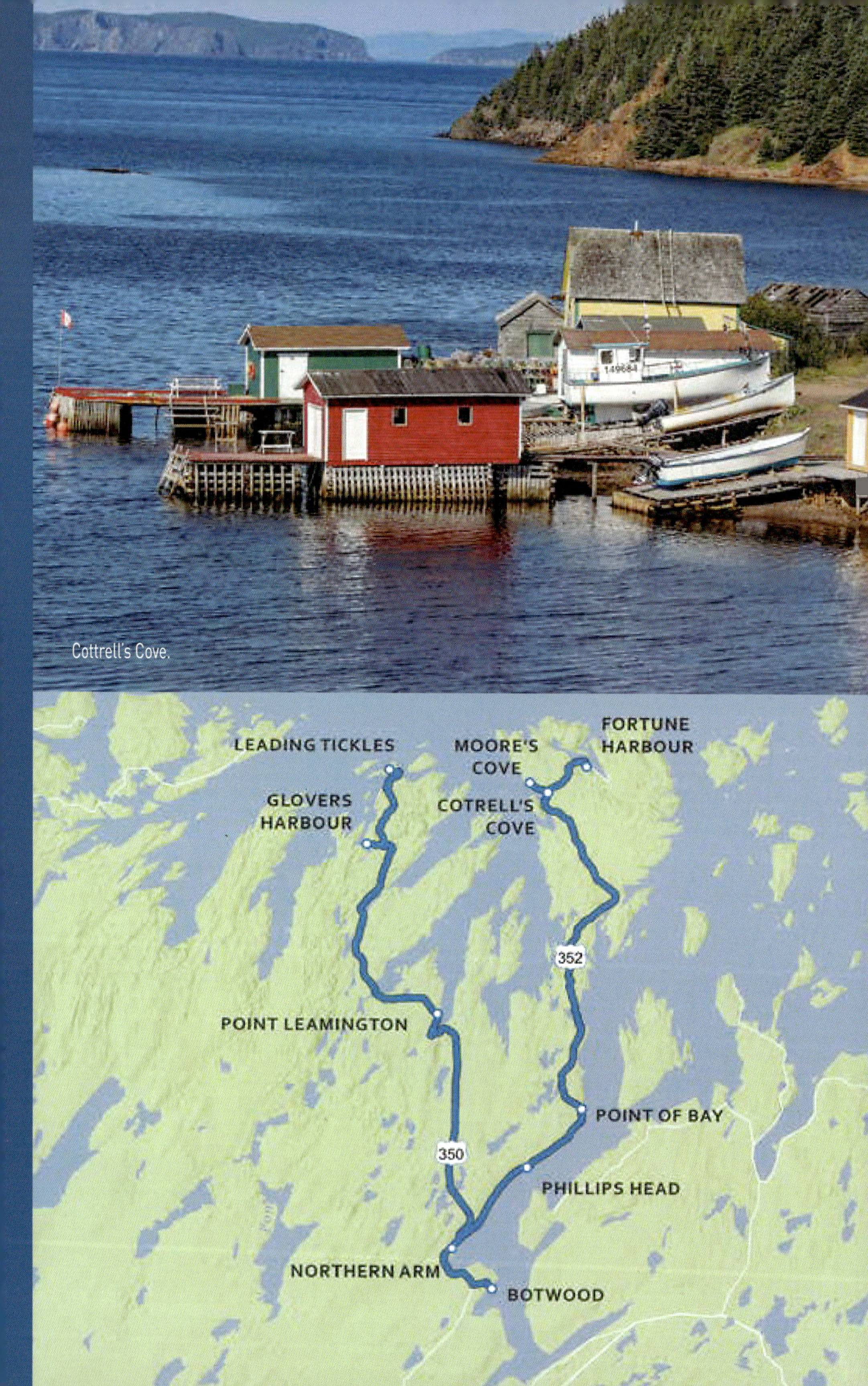

Cottrell's Cove.

> ❯ **Distance:** 234 km
> ❯❯ **Primary road(s):** Routes 350, 352
> ❯❯❯ **Amenities:** Botwood, Point Leamington

This trip starts in Botwood (population 2,778) and tours through communities along the Notre Dame Bay coastline in a 234-kilometre loop.

From Botwood, head southeast for 6 kilometres to Peterview (population 723), located on the Bay of Exploits. The first known inhabitants of Peterview, on Peters Arm, were the Beothuk who camped at Wigwam Point, a part of Sandy Point at the end of Peterview. When I was a kid, my family spent a lot of time at Wigwam Point, travelling around there in my father's 14-foot aluminum boat and eating meals my mother cooked on a Coleman stove for all 11 of us. Now I visit every year by motorcycle.

After a visit to Wigwam Point, return to Botwood, known for its deep harbour once favoured by cargo ships and seaplanes. In 1909, AND Company, owners of the Grand Falls paper mill, built a railway to Botwood to ship their newsprint around the world from Botwood harbour.

Botwood's aviation history begins in 1930 when the first transatlantic passenger flight left there for Ireland. During World War II, the RCAF used Botwood as a seaplane base and the remains of its massive concrete slipway are still being used in 2024. The history of the town is celebrated in over a dozen murals, maintained by the Botwood Mural Arts Society—these alone are reason enough to visit.

From Botwood, head northwest along Route 350 to

Church of St. Anne, Fortune Harbour.

Mural celebrating medical history, Botwood area.

Northern Arm (population 371). Pendragon Trail in Northern Arm leads to a gazebo—an excellent stop for birdwatchers—and continues to Evans Point. Watch for the trailhead on Route 350.

At the end of Northern Arm, Routes 350 and 352 intersect. Turn left onto Route 350 and ride about 21 kilometres to Point Leamington (population 574), spread along the shore of Southwest Arm on Notre Dame Bay. At the entrance to Point Leamington is access to Mill River, a large salmon river,

Life-sized 55-foot giant squid sculpture, Glovers Harbour.

Catalina Canso flying boat, Botwood.

alongside a day park and a trailer park. A glove manufacturing factory is a top local employer. Hikers can check out Rowsell's Nature Trail.

Continue on Route 350 north for 19 kilometres to a left turn into Glovers Harbour (population 55). This fishing community was once called Thimble Tickle; a giant squid was found on its shores in 1878 and recognized by the Guinness Book of World Records as the largest giant squid specimen ever recorded.

Glovers Harbour.

Return to Route 350 and ride to Leading Tickles (population 292). Part of this town is on Cull Island, connected to the mainland by a bridge. Look for icebergs in the spring. Camping is available at Ocean View Park.

Backtrack southward 48 kilometres to Northern Arm and the intersection with Route 352. Turn left and ride northward, through five fishing communities. Phillips Head, about 8 kilometres northeast of Northern Arm, has a World War II gun battery that protected the harbour of Botwood; the battery can be accessed via a 200-metre trail. Next along the route is Point of Bay (population 137), with its picturesque harbour. Thirty-one kilometres farther is Cottrell's Cove (population 123), then Moore's Cove, and, finally, Fortune Harbour.

From Fortune Harbour, ride 58 kilometres south to return to Botwood.

Leading Tickles.

Salmon fishers, Mill River, Point Leamington.

Cod splitting shed, Moore's Cove.

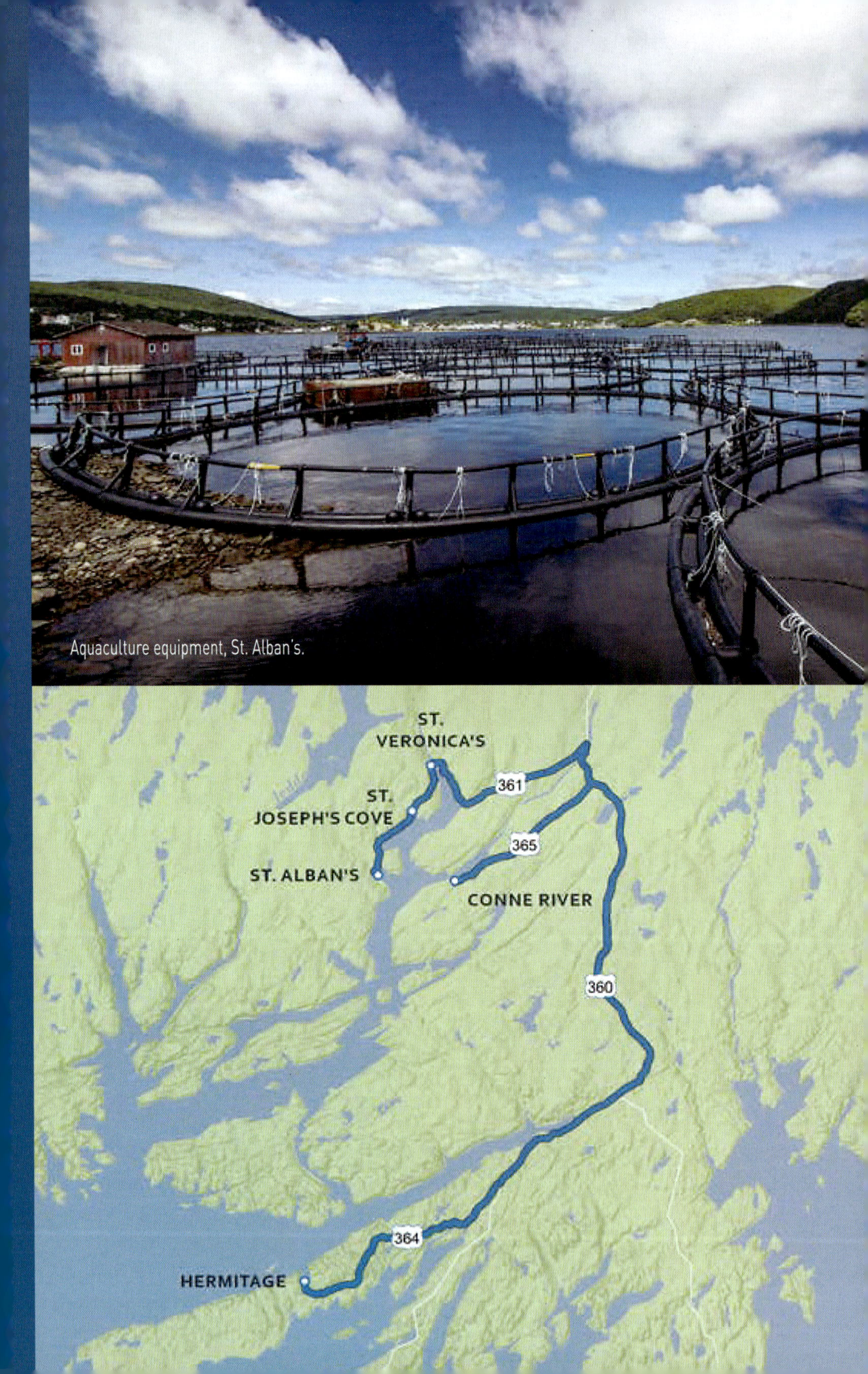

Aquaculture equipment, St. Alban's.

23 Connaigre Peninsula West plus Ferries

> **Distance:** 227 km
>> **Primary road(s):** Routes 360, 361, 364, 365
>>> **Amenities:** St. Alban's, Conne River, Hermitage

This trip covers the western side of the Connaigre Peninsula via a return trip from St. Alban's south to Hermitage, with the option for further exploration by coastal ferry.

St. Alban's (population 1,189), the largest community on Bay d'Espoir, was settled in the mid-1800s, though the French had timber rights in the area as far back as 1776. Originally named Ship Cove, it was a trading, fishing, and logging community; in 2024, it is known for hydro generation and aquaculture.

The Newfoundland Aquaculture Industry Association (NAIA) has an office in St. Alban's. St. Alban's also has a 58,000-square-foot fish health laboratory. The hydro generation site in the town is the largest on the island of Newfoundland.

From St. Alban's, ride north on Route 361 for 7 kilometres to the amalgamated town of St. Joseph's Cove-St. Veronica's. Continue another 17 kilometres northeast on Route 361 along Bay d'Espoir to the intersection with Route 360. Turn right and ride toward Hermitage and Seal Cove at the southwest coast of the peninsula.

Ride 4 kilometres, turn right onto Route 365 (road to Conne River), and continue 15 kilometres to the town of Conne River. In 1984, the Miawpukek Band was officially recognized as the Mi'kmaq First Nations band government in Conne River. In 2019, a registered population of 800 lived on the 36-square kilometre Miawpukek Band Reserve in Conne River Reserve,

McCallum.

Take advantage of these ferries while they are operational. Schedules are available at 511nl.ca or https://www.gov.nl.ca/ti/ferryservices/schedules/.

Crossing Times:

- Gaultois to Hermitage approximately 20 minutes (6 km)
- Gaultois to McCallum approximately 1.5 hours (27 km)
- McCallum to Hermitage approximately 1.5 hours (26 km)

Fog over Gaultois.

and another 2,200 people lived in the municipality of Conne River.

The Miawpukek Band celebrates its culture with an annual Powwow. The Powwow weekend is a feast of food, arts, crafts, and ceremony. The band also operates Jipujijkuei Kuespem Park, which is available for camping.

Backtrack to Route 360 and turn right (south). Ride 30 kilometres and exit onto Route 364 toward Hermitage.

The next 35 kilometres are through a landscape of mountains and fjords. Hermitage (population 189), in a well-protected harbour on Hermitage Bay, was once a French fishing port appreciated for being a deep ice-free harbour. As you enter Hermitage, a mussel farming operation is visible on the left.

If you have the time, take the passenger ferry out of Hermitage to Gaultois and McCallum. Leave your bike in the designated parking lot in Hermitage and take the ferry to Gaultois for overnight. The next morning you can ferry to McCallum and return to Hermitage that afternoon. Alternatively, visit one of these beautiful communities as a day trip.

From Hermitage, take the highway back to St. Alban's, for a total trip of 227 kilometres.

Fishing boats, Harbour Breton.

24

Connaigre Peninsula East plus Ferries

> **Distance:** 211 km
>> **Primary road(s):** Routes 360, 362, 363
>>> **Amenities:** Harbour Breton, English Harbour West

The Connaigre Peninsula seems off the beaten path, and many bikers don't make the trip—which is a shame, because the roads are well maintained and the scenery spectacular.

This trip starts in Harbour Breton and heads north around a horseshoe to Coomb's Cove and returns to Harbour Breton, with the optional add-on of a trip by passenger ferry to Rencontre East.

Harbour Breton (population 1,477), at the southern end of the Coast of Bays on the Connaigre Peninsula, is the hub for the peninsula, with shops, restaurants, and accommodations. Historically, the Newman Company had storage facilities for their port wine in Harbour Breton, employing as many as 100 in the late 1800s. It also salted, dried, and packaged fish for Europe, South America, and the Caribbean islands.

Fishing has long been the main source of employment in Harbour Breton. Fishery Products International operated fish plants there for years, but the Barry Group took them over in the early 2000s. Harbour Breton is also home to aquaculture facilities operated by the Norwegian company Mowi; the ice-free waters of the south coast of Newfoundland are suitable for fishing and fish farms.

Take Route 360 out of Harbour Breton for a ride through hills and alongside fjords. After riding in a northeasterly direction for about 38 kilometres, turn right onto Route 362 and head south.

About 8 kilometres along Route 362 is an intersection: turn left onto Harbour Drive and ride 8 kilometres to Pool's Cove. From this small aquaculture community (population 143), consider parking your bike in the designated parking lot and taking the 75-minute ferry ride to the isolated community of Rencontre East. Rencontre East is also accessible by ferry from Bay L'Argent on the Burin Peninsula to the east. For ferry schedules, visit 511nl.ca or https://www.gov.nl.ca/ti/ferryservices/schedules/.

Belleoram, from the highway.

On your return to Pool's Cove, backtrack the 8 kilometres to the intersection with Route 362. Ride about 20 kilometres to Route 363. Here, you can turn left onto Belleoram Road or right onto Coomb's Cove Road. Let's turn left. As you head east along Belleoram Road, the first community is St. Jacques, nestled around St. Jacques Harbour. Just 4 kilometres more and you'll arrive in Belleoram (population 348), around a large sheltered harbour the French originally called *Bande de Laurier*. In 1891, the Anglican St. Lawrence Church was built,

known as Cathedral of the South Coast among residents. Iron Skull Mountain is a local landmark and the namesake of the Iron Skull Festival, an annual celebration of music and food. The main industry in Belleoram is aquaculture.

From Belleoram, ride back on Belleoram Road for 8 kilometres to the intersection of Routes 363 and 362. Take Coomb's Cove Road (Route 363) to the communities of English Harbour West, Boxey, Wreck Cove, and Coomb's Cove. English Harbour West is a hub of commerce for communities east of Harbour Breton. After Boxey, ride 4 kilometres west to the right-hand exit toward the community of Wreck Cove. Wreck Cove is one of my favourite communities on the peninsula, for its beauty.

Return to Coomb's Cove Road and continue on to Coomb's Cove. From there, head back to Harbour Breton using Routes 363, 362, and 360 to finish this 211-kilometre run filled with bays, fjords, mountains, and picture-perfect communities.

Sunny Cottage tourism information centre, Harbour Breton.

Norris Arm Municipal Park.

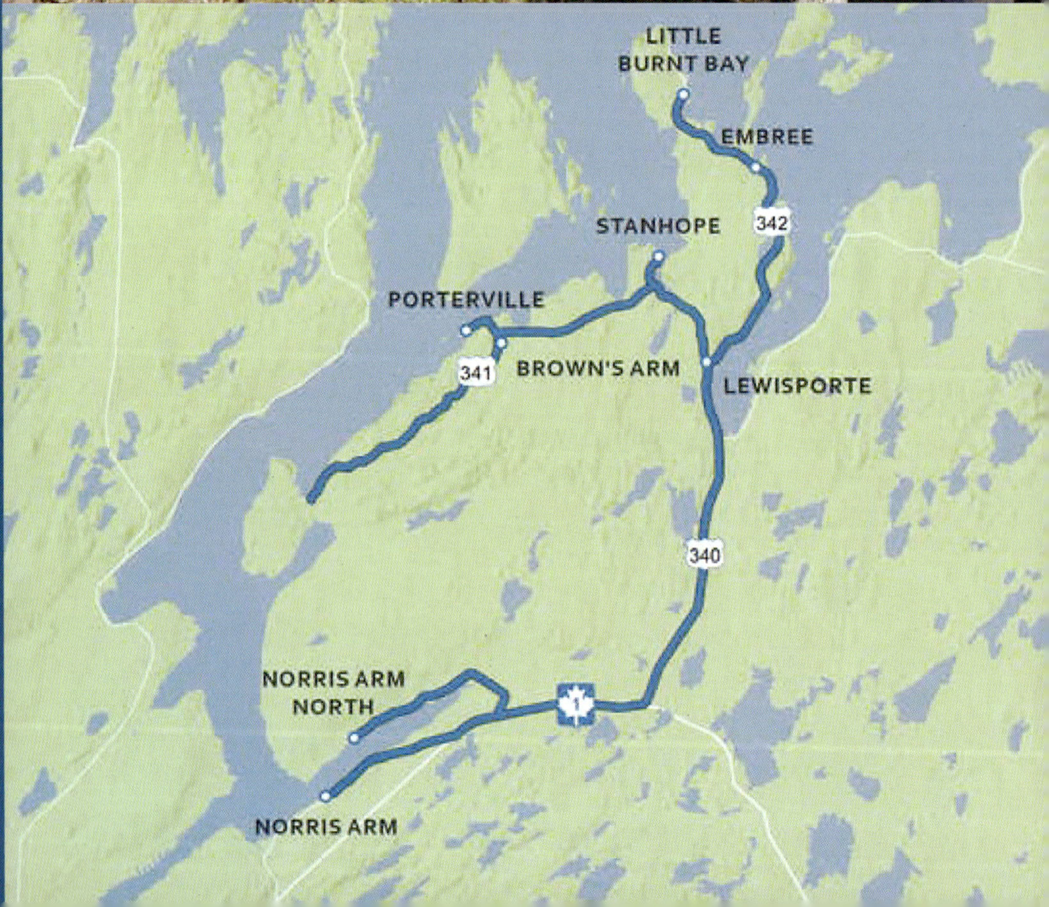

LITTLE
BURNT BAY
EMBREE
342
STANHOPE
PORTERVILLE
341
BROWN'S ARM
LEWISPORTE
340
NORRIS ARM
NORTH
NORRIS ARM

25

Bay of Exploits East
Norris Arm to Laurenceton

> **Distance:** 151 km
>> **Primary road(s):** TCH; Routes 340, 342, 341
>>> **Amenities:** Norris Arm, Lewisporte

This 151-kilometre return trip takes you through communities on the eastern side of the Bay of Exploits, beginning at the town of Norris Arm, at the mouth of the Exploits River.

The Norris Arm Heritage & Arts Centre on the waterfront in Norris Arm offers information about the area's aviation, railroad, logging, archaeology, and military history. Of the walking trails in the vicinity, I recommend Eel Brook Trail on the eastern side of town. On the western side of town is Norris Arm Municipal Park, a good place to enjoy fall colours, if you visit in season.

From Norris Arm, head to the TCH, ride east for 2 kilometres, then exit to the left toward Norris Arm North. Ride around the bay for 8 kilometres to Norris Arm North. Stop by Norris Arm North's lookout platform for a view of the Bay of Exploits and across the water toward Norris Arm.

Return to the TCH and ride east for 6 kilometres; take the Lewisporte exit (Route 340). You'll first arrive at Lewisporte Junction; from here, head north for 15 kilometres to the town of Lewisporte. You'll see the Lewisporte Train Park as you enter the town. Ride through Lewisporte on Route 340 (we'll return to Lewisporte for Trip 26) and turn left onto Route 341 (Premier Drive). The first community on Route 341 is Stanhope (population 280) on Stanhope Cove in the Bay of Exploits.

Continue back along Route 341 and turn right toward Brown's Arm. At the entrance to Brown's Arm is an intersection

Laurenceton.

by Maranatha Pentecostal Tabernacle. A 3-kilometre detour
to the right here leads to Porterville along the Bay of Exploits.

Return to Brown's Arm and take Route 341 to
Laurenceton and an 11-kilometre stretch of quiet, winding
road. You will pass logging roads used by residents to get
their winter wood, as well as several farms. Laurenceton
(population 183) is built around the picturesque Kite Cove.

Ride back toward Lewisporte for 21 kilometres to the
intersection with Route 342. Turn left toward Embree
and Little Burnt Bay. Embree is drive-through community
(population 679) about 10 kilometres north. Exit right on

Little Burnt Bay Harbour Authority.

Collins day park and museum, Embree.

Alex Lane in Embree to see two shipwrecks: ride up to a wharf and walk out to within 20 feet of the HMS *Calypso* and HMS *Briton*.

At the corner near the Collins Day Park and Museum in Embree is a 1967 Wolverine Bearcat snow machine with a wood sled that came from Botwood. It sits on a 1940s cargo cart that was used at the Gander Airport.

Five kilometres northwest of Embree is the end of Route 342 in Little Burnt Bay (population 238), with its well-maintained harbour authority at the end of the community. One year a beluga whale swam around in this harbour for days, much to the delight of people, including my wife and me.

From Little Burnt Bay, backtrack 43 kilometres through Lewisporte to the TCH and back to Norris Arm.

Inside the former Campbellton mill.

26 Lewisporte Loop

> **Distance:** 230 km
>> **Primary road(s):** TCH; Routes 330, 331, 340
>>> **Amenities:** Lewisporte, Gander, Gander Bay North

This 230-kilometre Lewisporte loop includes many exits and side trips.

Lewisporte Harbour is in Burnt Bay, part of the Bay of Exploits, which eventually opens into Notre Dame Bay. Lewisporte (population 3,300) has traditionally been home to logging, fishing, and shipbuilding industries. During World War II, three army sites in Lewisporte protected the fuel supply lines into the airport town of Gander. More recently, large wholesale businesses set up in Lewisporte to avail of its deepwater harbour and docks as a distribution centre, earning the town the title "Gateway to the North," thanks to the many supply ships that travelled northward from Lewisporte to Labrador. Today the Trans-Labrador Highway is the primary route used to supply Labrador.

At the entrance to Lewisporte, by the Tim Horton's coffee shop, turn right onto Route 340 and head northeast along Lewisporte Harbour toward Campbellton. Route 340 (Road to the Isles) leads northward to New World Island and Twillingate Islands (see Trip 27).

Leave Route 340 and turn onto Bob Clark Drive for a leisurely ride through Campbellton. Nearby Indian Arm River was once a Beothuk encampment; Campbellton was originally called Indian Arm but later renamed for sawmill manager John Campbell.

Backtrack and turn left onto Route 340. You'll pass the

Gander River boats, Gander Bay South.

ruins of a pulp mill close to the water. The Horwood Lumber Company pulp mill and hydro facility were built between 1911 and 1913 and began producing pulp in 1914.

Continue on Route 340 eastward to the exit to Comfort Cove-Newstead (Route 343). Turn left and head north for 15 kilometres into the community, which amalgamated Comfort Cove, Newstead, and Turtle Creek. Beothuk grave sites have been discovered in this area and it is assumed that the Beothuk were attracted there by plentiful fishing, as European settlers were.

Return to Route 340, turn left, and ride 12 kilometres to the exit to Baytona. Turn left again onto Main Street into Baytona. The 5 kilometres to and through Baytona is a relaxing ride up the western side of Birchy Bay.

Back on Route 340, ride 3 kilometres and turn left into the town of Birchy Bay. Continue through the town—this road takes you back to Route 340.

The next intersection is of Routes 340 and 331. Turn right onto Route 331 and head overland to Gander Bay. Ride 8 kilometres to a left turn into Horwood. The community

Glenwood train trestle with Gander River boat.

of Horwood (population 260), once called Dog Bay, was the home of a sawmill owned by the Horwood family. The Horwoods also owned and operated the Horwood Pulp Company in Campbellton.

Return to Route 331, turn left, and travel southeast 9 kilometres to the exit to Rodgers Cove, a small community with many seasonal cabins.

Backtrack to Route 331 out of Rodgers Cove and turn left to Wings Point and eventually to Clarke's Head. You'll next cross the 191-metre-long Gander Bay causeway to Gander Bay South. Turn onto Route 330 toward Gander.

One kilometre past the causeway, turn right onto River Loop Crescent, which takes you to Gander River and the Gander Bay River Loop Wharf. The short road to the wharf is a graded gravel road. At the wharf, you will notice the Gander River boat (also known as a Gander River canoe), a common boat on the 60-kilometre-long Gander River. Canoes are common on the river but the river boat—a hybrid of a canoe and a punt (small wooden boats used for inshore fishing)—is better suited for the large river with its rapids and its long ponds.

Oil/chemical tanker
QikiQtaaluk W., Lewisporte.

Return to Route 330 and head south for 41 kilometres to the town of Gander (we'll revisit Gander on Trip 30) and the intersection with the TCH. Turn right on the TCH to ride 22 kilometres to Appleton (population 620).

At the Riverfront Peace Park in Appleton is a piece of steel from the Twin Towers disaster of 9/11. This steel was presented to the town for hosting dozens of the passengers who were diverted into Gander during the attack in NYC.

Next on the TCH is the Queen Elizabeth II Bridge, constructed in 1953 and rebuilt in 2003. A train trestle crosses the Gander River parallel to the vehicle bridge. On the west side of the bridge is Glenwood, another small town which helped those stranded during 9/11. Lakewood Academy, the K-12 school in Glenwood, serves both Appleton and Glenwood.

Continue west on the TCH for 23 kilometres past Notre Dame Park and turn right onto Route 340 by Miracle Temple. From here, it is 12 kilometres back to Lewisporte.

Horwood Lumber Co. mill, Campbellton.

Inside the former mill.

Air Search and Rescue, Gander.

Pike's Arm.
CROW HEAD
DURRELL
BACK HARBOUR
PIKES ARM
HERRING NECK
TWILLINGATE
TOO GOOD
ARM
COBBS
ARM
TIZZARD'S
HARBOUR
346
HILLGRADE
VALLEY POND
MORETON'S
HARBOUR
345
340
COTTLESVILLE
SUMMERFORD
344
BOYDS COVE

27 New World Island and Twillingate Islands

> Distance: **215 km**
>> Primary road(s): **Routes 340, 344, 345, 346**
>>> Amenities: **Twillingate, Summerford**

Route 340, the Road to the Isles, leads from Lewisporte to Long Point Lighthouse on North Twillingate Island. The isles—New World Island, Twillingate Islands, Change Islands, and Fogo Island—are immortalized in the song "I'se the B'y": "Fogo, Twillingate, Moreton's Harbour / All around the circle."

Trip 27 travels on Route 340 from Boyd's Cove in the North Shore Forest ecoregion and heads north through New World Island to South Twillingate Island and North Twillingate Island, with side trips and diversions.

Boyd's Cove (population 183), also known as Boyd's Harbour, is home to the Boyd's Cove Beothuk Site, a provincial historic site. The interpretation centre reveals the culture and life of the Beothuks. A 1.5-kilometre walking trail from the centre leads to an 18th-century Beothuk village, the remains of which were discovered in 1981.

In the 19th century, families from Fogo Island settled in Boyd's Cove, where they fished, logged, and later farmed. The shoreline is protected from the open ocean by the many islands offshore, making it attractive to settlers.

From Boyd's Cove, head 14 kilometres along Route 340 to New World Island. Exit left onto Route 344 to Summerford (population 906). A fire hall, gas station, grocery store, and restaurant are located at this intersection. Summerford has long been known for fishing, logging, and farming. Less than

Manuel's Cove.

1 kilometre along Route 344 is a fork in the road: go left for a leisurely ride on Strong's Island in Summerford Arm.

Backtrack and ride along Route 344 to Cottlesville (population 244) in Luke's Arm.

Return to Summerford and exit left onto Route 340 for the next leg of this tour of New World Island.

Three kilometres north of Summerford is Virgin Arm-Carter's Cove (population 442). This is lobster country and, in season, you can buy fresh local lobster or have a restaurant lobster meal in most communities from here north to Twillingate.

Continue to Bridgeport, Moreton's Harbour, Valley Pond, and Tizzard's Harbour on Route 345. Along the way, you will traverse the three peninsulas of this part of New World Island.

The fishing community of Bridgeport (population 104) is spread over a series of hills and inlets. Next is Moreton's Harbour (population 28), about 2 kilometres farther north along Route 345. Four kilometres west of Moreton's Harbour is Valley Pond (originally Whale's Gulch, population 101). Return to Moreton's Harbour and ride 7 kilometres northeast to Tizzard's Harbour (population 55).

Ride 17 kilometres back to Virgin Arm via Route 345 and turn left on Route 340. The next community is Hillgrade; if you are craving a seafood meal, consider Doyle Sansome & Son Ltd. Restaurant.

Skipper Jim's tours, Gillard's Cove.

Head 6 kilometres north from Hillgrade and take the exit to Newville.

Back on Route 340, ride another 2 kilometres northeast to the Cobb's Arm exit, which takes you to the New World Island communities of Roger's Cove, Cobb's Arm, Toogood Arm, Green Cove, and Pike's Arm, in that order.

Backtrack 12 kilometres from Pike's Arm to Route 340. Head north for 1 kilometre and exit right onto Herring Neck Road. In 3 kilometres, you will reach Merritt's Harbour; in another 3 kilometres, Herring Neck. Herring Neck was once a thriving fishing community, but its population has dwindled since the cod moratorium of 1992.

Return to Route 340, turn right, and take the causeway to South Twillingate Island. On your immediate left after the

causeway is Prime Berth Twillingate Fishery and Heritage Centre, an interpretation centre focusing on Newfoundland and Labrador's connection to the fishery. Just past the centre is a left turn into Black Duck Cove. Before the causeway to South Twillingate Island was built in 1964, residents and visitors took a ferry between Black Duck Cove and Indian Cove on New World Island to get to the Twillingate Islands.

Return to Route 340 and ride north for 2 kilometres to the turn to Purcell's Harbour, a small drive-through community that takes only a few minutes to see before you are back on Route 340. One kilometre later, turn right to Little Harbour, another drive-through community. This community of about a dozen families has a few interesting wharves and, over the years, icebergs have often grounded in the harbour.

Continue on Route 340 into Twillingate and to the intersection with Main Street. Turn right toward Durrell. The road twists along the coastline for the next 3 to 5 kilometres, depending on how far you wish to go. In late spring and early summer, you'll likely see icebergs, but the coastline is picture-perfect all year long.

Bike back to the Twillingate intersection and onto Route 340, which leads through Twillingate to Long Point Lighthouse at the top of North Twillingate Island. On the way, take a side trip to scenic Back Harbour, then continue on through Crow Head (population 156) to Long Point Lighthouse.

Twillingate bills itself as the ultimate outport experience in Iceberg Alley: whale tours, hiking trails, kayaking, fresh seafood, coastal scenes, theatre, music, coffee shops, and the Split Rock Brewing Company. If you have time, it is an ideal place to get off your bike and stay awhile.

To return to Boyd's Cove, leave Route 340 and turn right onto Rink Road. This becomes Bayview Street and winds through the communities of Gillard's Cove, Manuel's Cove, and Kettle Cove and back onto Route 340. Head south for a 38-kilometre ride to Boyd's Cove.

Tizzard's Harbour, with Twillingate Island in the background.

Back Harbour.

Lobster traps, Moreton's Harbour.

Newfoundland Pony Sanctuary, Change Islands.

28 Change Islands

> **Distance:** 67 km
>> **Primary road(s):** Route 335
>>> **Amenities:** Change Islands, Stoneville

A one-day trip to Change Islands

Trip 28 begins in the drive-through community of Stoneville; it has a gas station and convenience store. As you ride through Stoneville, you are on Route 335, headed to the Farewell ferry terminal.

If you have time before catching the ferry, go to Port Albert (population 66), less than 1 kilometre north of the ferry exit. This community is wrapped around Little Beaver Cove.

After a look around Port Albert, return to Route 335 and turn left onto the road to Farewell. Note: Farewell is not a community. There are washroom facilities but no food services; you may want to bring snacks and drinks if you expect a long wait. The ferry from the Farewell terminal to Change Islands takes about 20 minutes.

Your first stop after disembarking at Change Islands is the Newfoundland Pony Sanctuary, about 8 kilometres up the road. Newfoundland ponies are critically endangered. There's a barn on site

Trip 28 (Change Islands) and Trip 29 (Fogo Island) both begin at the northern part of Route 335 at the Farewell ferry next to Port Albert in Hamilton Sound, Notre Dame Bay. To explore these islands, you have three options:

- **Option 1)** Trip 28 to Change Islands can be completed leisurely in one summer day.
- **Option 2)** Trip 29 to Fogo Island can also be completed leisurely in one summer day.
- **Option 3)** Both Change Islands and Fogo Island can be covered in one longer (12-hour+) summer day—if you schedule your ferry rides to make it all happen. To do this, take the first ferry from Farewell to Change Islands in the morning, catching the ferry from Change Islands to Fogo around noon, and then returning to Farewell in the evening. Check the ferry schedules, as these vary from day to day and year to year.

Change Islands.
Stoneville.
Change Islands.
Change Islands.
Port Albert.

and almost always ponies in the large open-air corrals. Pony and buggy rides are available on summer days; a $5 donation buys a bale of hay for winter feedings.

Continue along the main road from the pony sanctuary toward the community of Change Islands (population 184). Change Islands comprises three islands, but the northern island is not accessible by bike. The two lower islands are populated and are separated by a strait of water called Main Tickle.

Before heading across the bridge over the tickle, turn left for a short drive past wharves and sheds, or turn right for a 5-kilometre ride along the coastline. Change Islands is known for its traditional homes, stages, and stores (fishing sheds).

As you leave South Change Islands, you cross the bridge onto Middle Change Islands. Stop by The Olde Shoppe Museum for a storyteller's tour through Newfoundland's past.

Other than lapping waves, an occasional ATV or motorboat sound, or chirping birds, the atmosphere is quiet and serene. These islands are lovely to walk or ride though and are a photographer's paradise. Take time to walk the 2-kilometre Squid-Jigger's Trail along the coast and immerse yourself in the landscape.

Well-known Newfoundlanders from Change Islands include artist Gerald Squires, writer Art Scammell, and Canon George Earle.

When you're ready to leave Change Islands, return to the ferry dock the way you came.

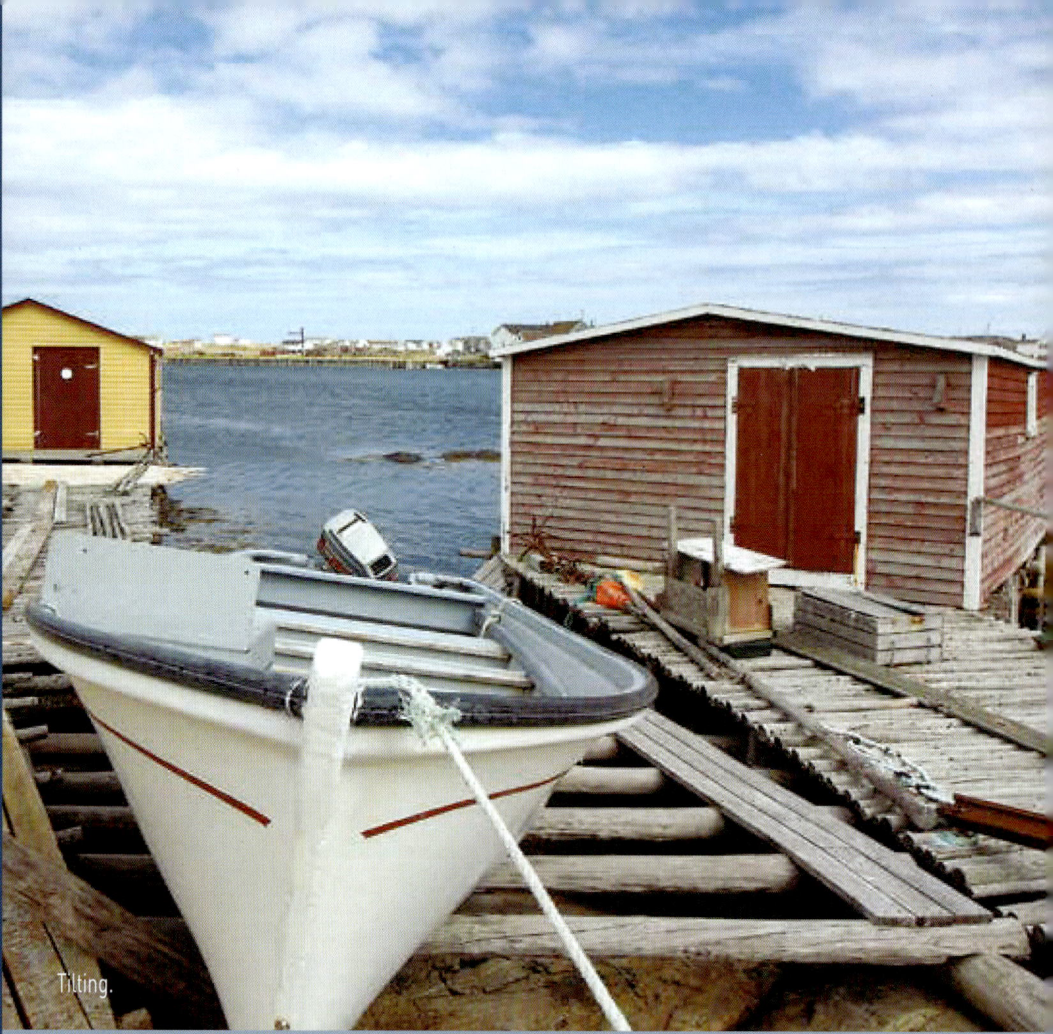

Tilting.

JOE BATT'S ARM
BARR'D ISLANDS
FOGO
TILTING
334
DEEP BAY
SHOAL BAY
ISLAND HARBOUR
333
FERRY TERMINAL
STAG HARBOUR

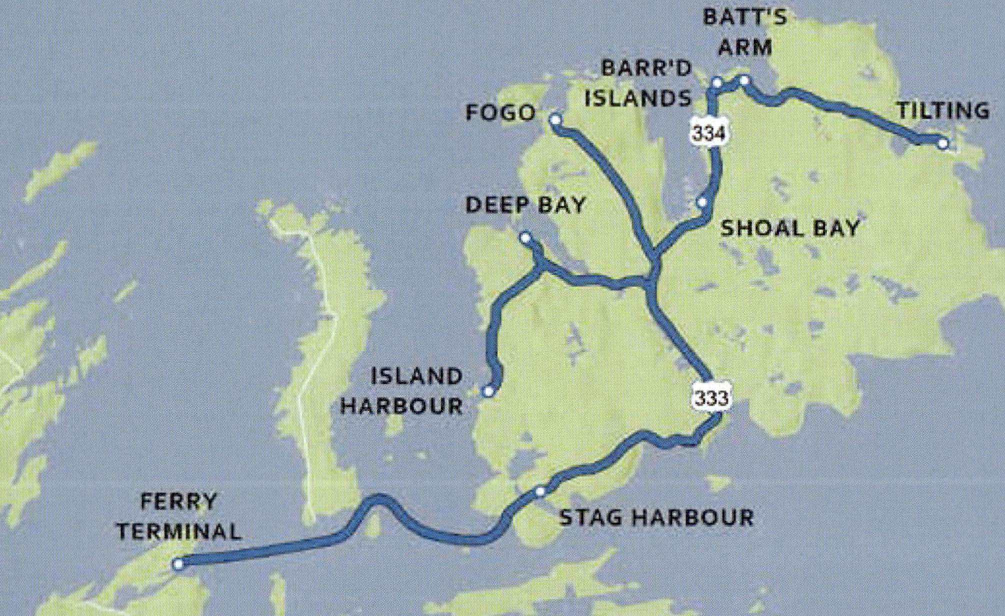

29 Fogo Island

> Distance: **140 km**
>> Primary road(s): **Routes 333, 334**
>>> Amenities: **Fogo, Tilting, Joe Batt's Arm**

The ferry trip from Farewell to Fogo Island is about 55 minutes and 14 kilometres. Be sure to consult the ferry schedule as you plan your trip (schedules are available at 511nl.ca).

Fogo Island (population 2,244) is the largest of Newfoundland's offshore islands, at 25 kilometres long and 14 kilometres wide. Its ties to England and Ireland are strong, especially in Tilting, where Irish dialects are still heard. French fishers were also early visitors; maps calling Fogo *Ile des Fougues* date to the 16th through the 18th centuries. Of course, the Beothuk used the island for sealing and fishing centuries before these European settlers.

Traditionally, the primary industry of Fogo was cod fishing and salting. The Fogo Island Co-operative Society formed in 1967 still operates three fish plants and a store in Seldom Come By. After the moratorium on cod fishing in 1992, the co-operative began handling crab, lobster, and many other species.

Tourism is the modern key to the livelihood of Fogo Island. Its hiking trails are legendary. Shorefast Foundation—a charity started by Fogo Island native Zita Cobb with the goal of building economic and cultural resilience on Fogo Island—operates the luxury Fogo Island Inn, as well as Fogo Island Arts, Fogo Island Fish, and other community and cultural enterprises.

Many icebergs pass by Fogo as they travel Iceberg Alley on the strong Labrador current. Other attractions include

Brimstone Head Folk Festival, the Flat Earth Society Museum, and the annual Great Fogo Island Punt Race. The punt, a small wooden fishing boat, takes on a new life with this annual event. Ethridge's Point Seaside Fest in Joe Batt's Arm is also a popular music festival.

About 11 kilometres from the ferry landing on Route 333 is the deep-harbour port of Seldom Come By. Ride 5 kilometres northwest on Route 333 and turn left into the communities of Deep Bay and Island Harbour. En route you pass the Fogo Aerodrome, where flights to the island land and take off.

Deep Bay (population 83) has a 1-kilometre hiking trail that offers expansive views of the area and the ocean. From Deep Bay, ride to Island Harbour (population 123).

Return to Route 333 and ride 1 kilometre north to reach the "middle" of Fogo Island: the intersection of Routes 333 and 334 and the location of the Cod Jigger Diner, Iceberg Arena, public library, Fogo Island Academy, RCMP station, and the Fogo health centre and pharmacy. From this junction, follow Route 333 to the town of Fogo or take Route 334 east toward Shoal Bay, Barr'd Islands, Joe Batt's Arm, and Tilting.

We'll take Route 334 first and ride east toward Tilting. The first community is Shoal Bay, home to one of five off-grid artist's studios run by the Shorefast Foundation—watch for a small building by the coast, built to evoke the shape of a humpback whale breaching. Artists from around the world apply for residency at these studios; their work is often displayed in the Fogo Island Gallery. The artist's retreat in Shoal Bay, Tower Studio, boasts a loft and a rooftop terrace and is connected to the main road by a long wooden boardwalk.

Continue on Route 334 to Barr'd Islands, settled by English fishers in 1836, and then Joe Batt's Arm. Joe Batt's Point Walking Trail passes another artist's studio and along the coast to a bronze statue of the extinct Great Auk. The 4.6-kilometre round trip trail starts at Etheridge's Point Park.

Joe Batt's Arm is home to the Fogo Island Inn, designed by Norwegian Todd Saunders and filled with Newfoundland-made décor and furniture.

Change Islands-Fogo Island ferry.

Squish Studio artist retreat, Tilting.

Fogo Island Inn, Joe Batt's Arm.

Seldom Come By.

Ride 9 kilometres to the southeast on Route 334 to Tilting, a community designated a national historic site of Canada and a registered heritage district by the Heritage Foundation of Newfoundland and Labrador, due to its preservation of 18th-century Irish landscape, buildings, and farming traditions, including fenced gardens. A cemetery in Tilting may be the oldest existing Irish cemetery in North America. Tilting has amalgamated with other communities into the town of Fogo, but all these communities, perhaps most notably Tilting, still showcase their individuality.

Return to the middle of the island via Route 334. Turn right at Fogo Island Academy and continue on Route 333 into the town of Fogo. Take the 2-kilometre walking trail to the top of Brimstone Head, an outcropping designated one of the four corners of the world, for a panoramic view of the town and the seascape.

Memorial United Church, Barr'd Islands.

Town of Fogo.

The town of Fogo is the starting point for several walking and hiking trails. It also has grocery stores, accommodations, and restaurants.

From the town of Fogo, return to the ferry terminal on Route 333.

Based on how long you want to explore Fogo Island—and considering ferry schedules—you can design a day trip to suit you.

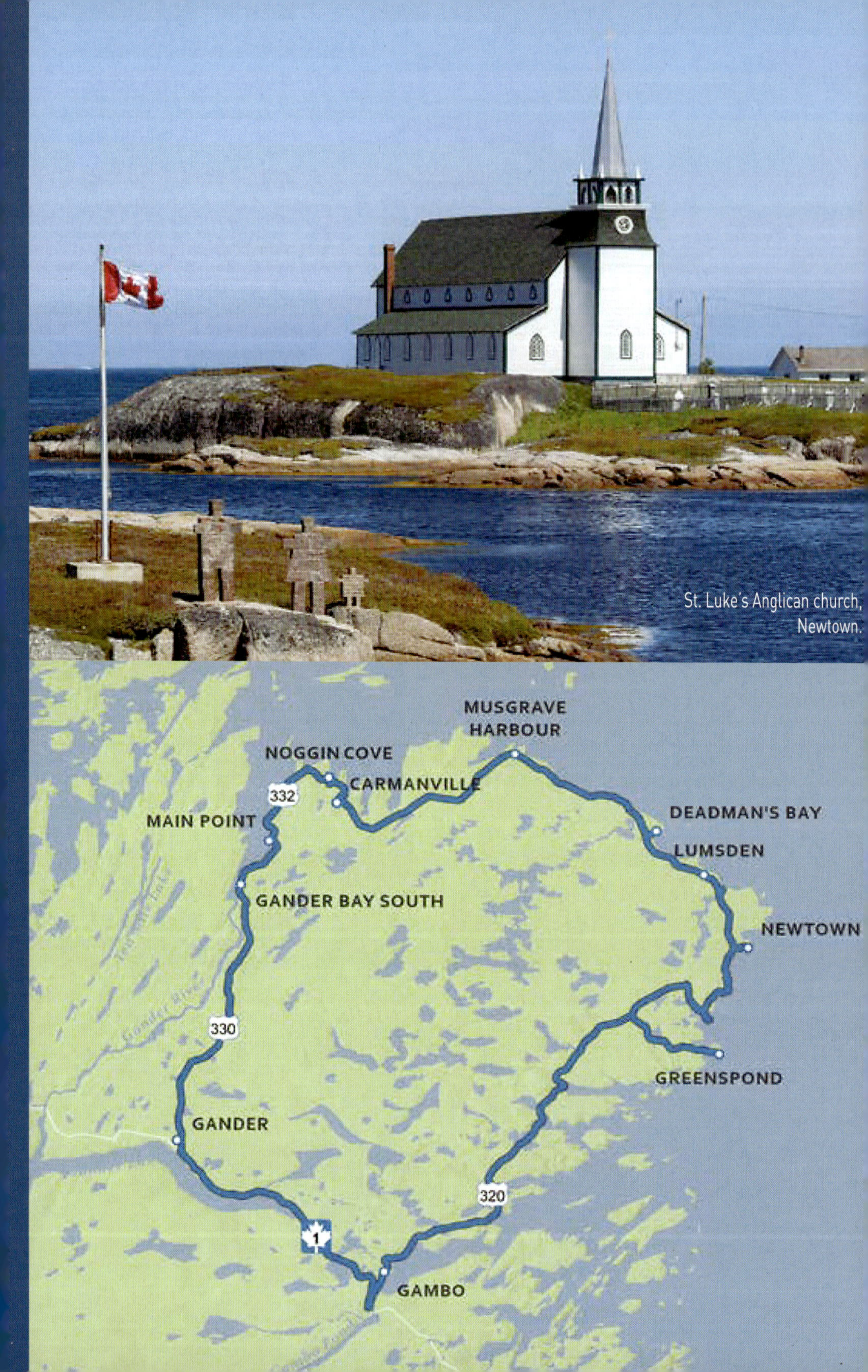

St. Luke's Anglican church, Newtown.

(30) Gander Loop

> Distance: **343 km**
>> Primary road(s): **Routes 320, 330, 332**
>>> Amenities: **Gander, Gambo, Musgrave Harbour, Wesleyville**

Gander to Gander … with lots of coastline in between

This 343-kilometre ride will lead you from the town of Gander north to Gander Bay to the communities on Hamilton Sound to the Straight Shore to communities along the western side of Bonavista Bay to Gambo and back on the TCH to Gander.

Gander (population 11,880) is home to the Gander International Airport. Once a critical refuelling stop for transatlantic air travel, it is still on call for emergency or medical issues. In 2001, 6,700 people were diverted to Gander on 38 aircraft in the wake of the 9/11 terrorist attack on New York. The hit Broadway show Come From Away is based on the event.

The aviation history of Gander is seen throughout the town, in everything from street names to the North Atlantic Aviation Museum. Air travel-related tragedies are recognized at memorial sites, including the Silent Witness Site commemorating the fatal losses at the Arrow Air Crash of 1985. Gander was well used by the Allied forces through World War II, when the town was called the "Crossroads of the World." As well, a large runway in Gander was designated an alternate landing site for the American Space Shuttle program.

Start your ride on Route 330 north out of Gander. In 42 kilometres, you will reach Harris Point, where you can get gas and supplies for your day. Do not cross the Gander Bay causeway on your left; instead, stay on Route 330 toward Main Point and Carmanville.

Badger's Quay root cellar.

Ride 8 kilometres to a left turn onto Route 332 toward Main Point and Davidsville for a 4-kilometre diversion to these small outport communities.

Return to Route 330 and ride 6 kilometres to the exit to Route 332 toward Carmanville (population 784). Carmanville is part of the Kittiwake Coast, which runs along a horseshoe-shaped shoreline. Fishing and shipbuilding have long been important to Carmanville's economy. The Wetlands Interpretation Centre and Nature Trail is worth a stop. The area is also popular for skiing, snowshoeing, salmon fishing, and birdwatching.

Return to Route 330 and ride 31 kilometres to Musgrave Harbour. Along this stretch of coastline, Hamilton Sound is on your left. Locally, this northeast coast is better known as the Straight Shore.

Deadman's Bay beach.

Lumsden Beach.

Gander International Airport.

Musgrave Harbour (population 946) has 7 kilometres of white, sandy beaches. The Fishermen's Museum and Banting Memorial Municipal Park are its main tourist attractions. Banting, the co-discoverer of insulin, died in a plane crash in 1941 near Musgrave Harbour. In the winter, ice fishing is popular in this area.

From Musgrave Harbour, ride Route 330 for 21 kilometres to a left-hand exit to Deadman's Bay (population 130). This area boasts fishing grounds and sandy beaches. I have also seen icebergs in this area.

Return to Route 330, turn left and ride 10 kilometres to Lumsden (population 535). Here a large wrap-around breakwater shelters fishing boats, the fish plant, and tourist boats. The whole of the Straight Shore is full of wonderful sandy beaches and those in Lumsden are particularly spectacular.

Back on Route 330 is Windmill Bight Park, a perfect spot to camp and enjoy a day of sun, beach, hiking, or fishing.

Another 11 kilometres along Route 330 is a left turn into Newtown (population 400). Settlers, mostly from Pinchard's Island, began coming to Newtown around 1850, where they built homes on the small islands in the area. They fished in the Labrador Straits and were involved with the local sealing industry.

The Barbour family of fishers and sealing captains came to Newtown at about the same time. These families became the main merchants of Newtown; their lives are celebrated at the Barbour Living Heritage Village.

Barbour Living Heritage Village, Newtown.

Musgrave Harbour.

Back on Route 330, ride 5 kilometres south where the road becomes Route 320. Instead of continuing straight, turn left onto a loop road called Route 26 which will bring you through Wesleyville, Brookfield, Badger's Quay, Pool's Island, and Valleyfield and eventually to Route 320.

Button's Landing display, Greenspond.

Harris Point.

Once you're back on Route 320, ride 9 kilometres to the left-hand exit onto Greenspond Road. Turn and ride 15 kilometres to Greenspond (population 257). Settlers came to this part of the island from the West Country of England in the 1690s.

Fishers from Greenspond have been cod fishing from their town up to the Labrador coast for centuries. Because of the northern ice floes on its coast, the area's fishers have also taken part in the yearly seal hunt. In 1873, a lighthouse erected on Puffin Island allowed seafarers to find this fishing community. In the early 20th century, a Union Trading Store, operated by the Fishermen's Protective Union, opened in Greenspond.

Return to Route 320 and head southwest toward Indian Bay, Wareham, Centreville, Trinity, and Hare Bay. This relaxing 23-kilometre ride along Bonavista Bay has plenty of restaurants and gas stations.

From Hare Bay, ride 19 kilometres to Gambo to finish Route 320 at the TCH. Gambo lies on Freshwater Bay, part of the larger Bonavista Bay. Next door in Mint Brook is where Joey Smallwood, former premier of Newfoundland and father of Confederation, was born. Mint Brook has amalgamated with communities in the area to officially become Dark Cove-Middle Brook-Gambo, with a population of 1,816.

The Logger's Memorial Park in Gambo celebrates the town's traditional industries. Logging artifacts as well as carved wooden life-sized loggers are on site. In the middle of town on Riverview Drive is a bronze statue of Smallwood by Bulgarian sculptor Luben Boykov. A nearby café also has a Smallwood statue. Stop at David Smallwood Park to stretch your legs on its scenic trails.

Just above the town of Gambo on the TCH is a parking lot overlooking Gambo and Freshwater Bay, aptly called "Joey's Lookout."

Now that you're back on the TCH, ride 40 kilometres northwest back to Gander.

Salvage.
HAYWARD'S
COVE
ST. BRENDAN'S
SHALLOWAY
COVE
BURNSIDE
ST.
CHADS
SALVAGE
GLOVERTOWN
CULLS
HARBOUR
32
310
TRAYTOWN
EASTPORT
TCH
HAPPY ADVENTURE
SANDY COVE

31 Eastport Peninsula plus Ferry

> **Distance:** 105 km
>> **Primary road(s):** TCH; Routes 32, 310
>>> **Amenities:** Glovertown, Eastport

Seven communities are located on the Eastport Peninsula in Bonavista Bay; a ferry runs from Burnside on the peninsula to Cottel Island, which is home to Shalloway Cove, St. Brendan's, and Hayward's Cove. Trip 31 is a ride around the entire peninsula, starting in Glovertown, on Route 310 (Road to the Beaches).

Glovertown (population 1,948) was originally called Bloody Bay and then Alexander Bay in 1894. Later it was renamed Glovertown after Sir John Hawley Glover, a governor of Newfoundland. Fishing, logging, and boat building have long been prosperous industries in this part of the province.

Leaving Glovertown on Route 310, ride 5 kilometres to Traytown. As you reach the far end of Traytown around cabin country, exit left toward Culls Harbour. You must cross a bridge which can only accommodate one line of traffic, so exercise caution. Once across the bridge, continue 3 kilometres on the paved Main Road through this quiet and picture-perfect community.

Backtrack across the bridge and turn left onto Route 310. Ride 4 kilometres along the edge of Terra Nova National Park to the Eastport causeway, which will take you to the Eastport Peninsula. An 11-kilometre stretch to the town of Eastport passes parks, restaurants, and other businesses. Harold Duffett Shriners Park, a fully serviced 147-site RV park, is busy all summer long.

Before we explore Eastport (population 527) and its sandy

Eastport causeway.

beaches, we'll take an exit from the town toward St. Brendan's on Cottel Island. As soon as you enter Eastport, watch for the left turn onto Legion Road (Route 32), which heads north toward St. Chad's, Burnside, and the St. Brendan's ferry. This 9-kilometre detour from Eastport to Burnside is worth the ride. At the 6-kilometre mark of Route 32 is a road into St. Chad's. This community was once called Damnable; according to folklore, it was named after a "damn bell" that was accidently struck by a pirate on a ship trying to hide out from a British ship outside the harbour.

Continue to Burnside (named because of a large fire that devastated the area in 1912), the most northerly community on Route 32. A number of channels and coves are located throughout Burnside; over time, places such as Squid Island were adjoined to Burnside by small bridges. Burnside has always been known for its fishing enterprises (salmon, herring, mackerel, cod, and squid).

As of 2024, a provincial ferry makes the 18-kilometre trip from Burnside to Cottel Island (population 125) three times a day.

Salvage.
Sandy Cove.
MV Grace Sparkes, Burnside.
St. Chad's.

Humpback whale near our fishing boat outside Salvage.

You can bring your motorcycle on the ferry to Cottel Island, but be prepared for mostly gravel roads on the other side.

After Burnside and/or Cottel Island, return to Eastport via Route 32. Eastport has B&Bs, cottages, and campsites to accommodate travellers who come to the area for the sandy beaches, scenery, hiking trails, events, and its proximity to Terra Nova National Park.

From Eastport, ride the last 9 kilometres of Route 310 northeast to the town of Salvage (population 108). There are walking trails all the way along the coastline from Eastport out to Salvage. Beothuks, Maritime Archaic people, and Groswater and Dorset people have been in this area as far back as five centuries ago.

The two main harbours in Salvage are Salvage Harbour and Bishop's Harbour. From these, fishers have plied their trades of fishing and sealing along their own coastline as well as on the Labrador Straits.

Head back to Eastport and on to the coastal communities of Happy Adventure and Sandy Cove. Happy Adventure (population 118) has a restaurant and other amenities, and Sandy Cove (population 120) is home to Sandy Cove Beach. From Sandy Cove, return to the TCH via Eastport and then back to Glovertown.

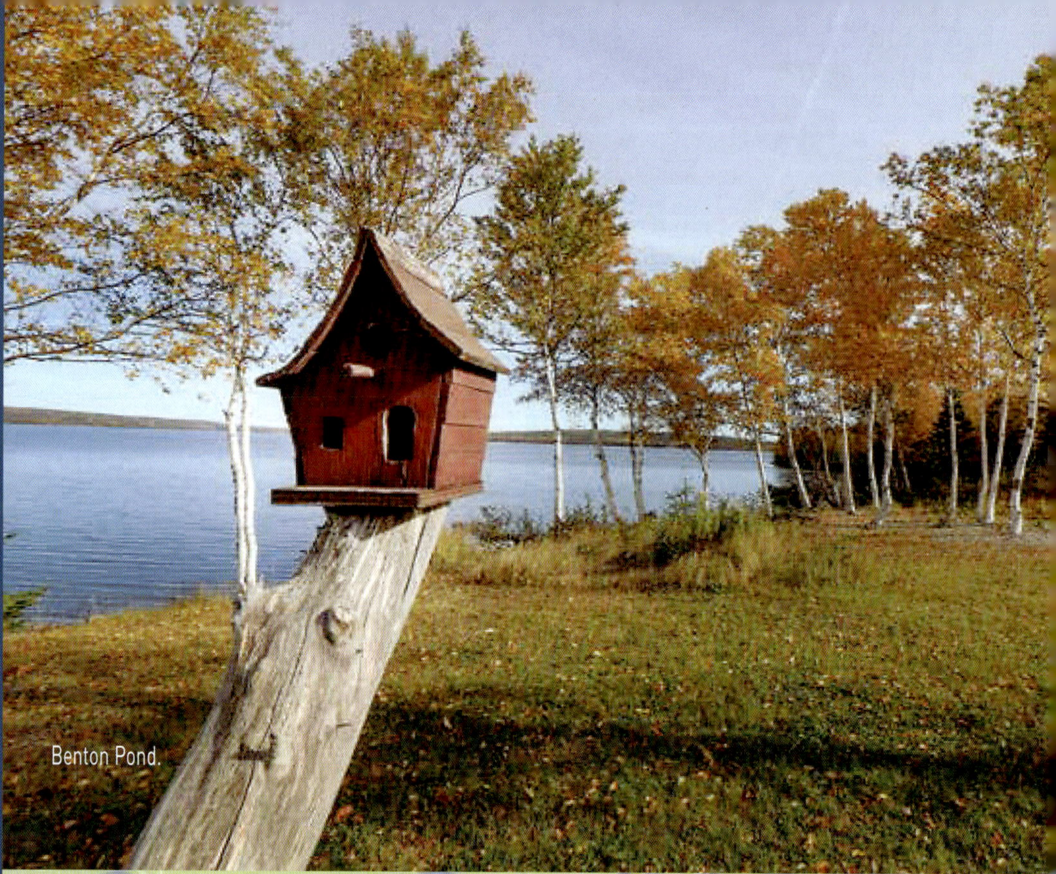

Benton Pond.

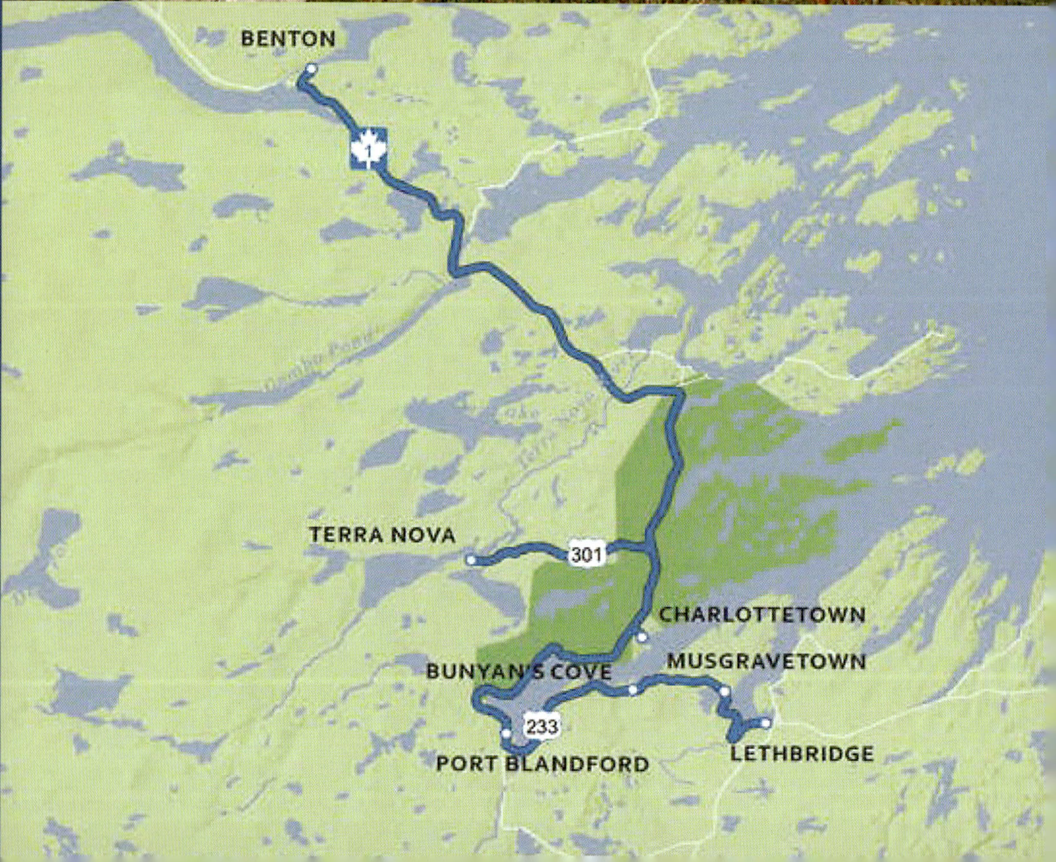

32 Terra Nova National Park and Environs

Benton to Lethbridge

> Distance: **312 km**
>> Primary road(s): **TCH; Routes 233, 234, 301**
>>> Amenities: **Port Blandford, Lethbridge**

This trip from Benton (east of Gander) through the Terra National Park out to Lethbridge in Bonavista Bay and back to Benton takes a minimum of 3 hours.

Start at the Benton TCH exit, approximately 18 kilometres east of Gander. A 2-kilometre ride from the TCH takes you to the heart of this community of 154 people. The Newfoundland railway was significant to Benton's history. Benton's sawmill and granite quarry were both made viable because the railway passed through the community. In fact, many of Benton's original inhabitants worked for the railway. A fence running along a personal property adjacent to the railbed commemorates Bob Osmond, who worked with the railway for 40 years. The community of Benton is bordered by Benton Pond, a cabin and cottage area.

Return to the TCH and ride 52 kilometres southeast to Terra Nova National Park. Along the way, you'll pass Gambo (see Trip 30) and the exit to Glovertown (Trip 31). Continue on the TCH south through the national park and enjoy a few diversions: parks, lookouts, and picnic areas.

Terra Nova National Park covers 399 square kilometres, including the coastal inlets of Bonavista Bay and mountains which are part of the Appalachians. The park offers hiking, canoeing, and kayaking, as well as opportunities to learn about the area's geology, animal, and bird life. Newman Sound and Malady Head campgrounds are available for tenting.

Clode Sound, Bunyan's Cove.

Seventeen kilometres from the entrance to Terra Nova National Park is a right turn into Terra Nova. The town, a 17-kilometre ride from the TCH, is not in the park and it is known for its trails and recreational fishing.

Eight kilometres from the exit to Terra Nova is the turn-off to Charlottetown. The Clode Sound Motel and Restaurant in Charlottetown is an option for a place to stay while you savour the park's highlights.

From the Charlottetown exit, ride 20 kilometres to the end of the national park and the golf greens of the Twin Rivers Golf Course, part of the Terra Nova Golf Resort, on both sides of the TCH. Six kilometres south is a left-hand exit into the community of Port Blandford and the entrance into the Terra

Nova Golf Resort, which has a 9-hole and an 18-hole golf course, considered one of the top courses in Atlantic Canada.

The Port Blandford Heritage Society has created a dozen storyboards around town to tell the history of the region. One is about the railway speeder, used to inspect tracks or to conduct surveys on or near the railway tracks. These speeders were also used to watch for small fires potentially started by friction caused by a bigger train on the tracks.

From Port Blandford, travel south on the TCH for 1 kilometre, then take a left-hand exit onto Route 233. Now you'll have the chance to slow down the pace and ride your bike for 34 kilometres along some of the small inlets and fertile farmlands of Bonavista Bay.

Railway speeder, Port Blandford.

Yurts, Malady Head, Terra Nova National Park.

Train mural, Benton.

Looking out Bonavista Bay from Charlottetown.

About 15 kilometres along this scenic road is Bunyan's Cove, located in a small cove on the south side of Clode Sound, Bonavista Bay. Ride another 9 kilometres along Route 233 to Musgravetown (population 561). This town was originally named Muddy Hole but the governor of Newfoundland, Sir Anthony Musgrave, had the name changed. Farms in this area specialize in dairy, poultry, and root vegetables. Malcolm Brown Memorial Park includes a sandy beach, campsites, and hiking trails. Accommodations are available in the area. A large United Church in Musgravetown was destroyed by fire in 1912 and rebuilt in 1913—you can't miss it.

As you near Lethbridge, you are approaching the Cabot Highway, which leads to Bonavista. Farming and forestry are the main industries of this area. The main crops are potatoes, carrots, turnips, and cabbage. Berry farming is also significant in this area and, as well, there are beef and turkey farms.

From Lethbridge, return to the TCH via Routes 233 and 234 and then on to Benton.

Lower Lance Cove, Random Island.
JAMESTOWN
PORTLAND
WINTER BROOK
234
BROOKLYN
MILTON
MONROE
232
NEW BURNT COVE
231
PETLEY
LOWER LANCE COVE
CLARENVILLE
ELLIOTT'S COVE
BRITANNIA
HICKMAN'S HARBOUR
LADY COVE

Random Island and Surroundings
Clarenville to Winter Brook

> **Distance: 221 km**
>> **Primary road(s): Routes 231, 232, 234**
>>> **Amenities: Clarenville**

Trip 33 goes from Clarenville in Trinity Bay to Winter Brook in Bonavista Bay. Clarenville (population 6,700), located on the TCH, is a service and supply hub for 96,000 people in 90 communities within a 100-kilometre radius. It is also home to White Hills Ski Resort, which offers downhill skiing, Nordic skiing, snowshoeing, and cross-country skiing.

As you leave TCH and ride into Clarenville, you reach Random Sound in the lower part of town.

This deep ice-free port is suitable for commercial shipping. From Clarenville, ride 3 kilometres north on Memorial Drive to Shoal Harbour. Continue north for another 3 kilometres on Balboa Drive to Milton. Adjacent to Cabot Timbermart's parking lot is a right-hand turn toward Random Island on Route 231 (Random Island Road). Turn onto Route 231 and cross the causeway to Random Island.

The main road on Random Island is about 74 kilometres return, passing the communities of Lady Cove, Hickman's Harbour, Britannia, Lower Lance Cove, and Petley. Lady Cove, on the southwest coast of Random Island, faces into Random Sound.

Eight kilometres farther up the road is a right turn onto Main Road, leading to Hickman's Harbour. Its deep harbour makes it ideal for fishing and shipbuilding industries.

Return to Random Island Road and ride 4 kilometres northeast to Britannia, on the Smith Sound side of Random

Waterville, Smith Sound.

Golden Shell Fisheries, Hickman's Harbour.

Clarenville marina, Random Sound.

Island, which offers a clear view across Smith Sound and Trinity Bay.

Take Main Road out of Britannia and travel 1 kilometre east along the coast to Lower Lance Cove.

Return to Britannia and ride northwest on Random Island Road for 5 kilometres to Petley, another picturesque community on Smith Sound. One of its attractions is its busy marina.

A 30-minute ride from Petley brings you back to the Random Island Causeway and Milton. Ride 4 kilometres north of Milton on Main Road to the intersection with Route 232. Turn right and ride along the north shore of Smith Sound through Monroe (named for a former prime minister of the Dominion of Newfoundland, Walter Stanley Monroe), Waterville, Clifton, Burgoyne's Cove, and New Burnt Cove on a 58-kilometre return trip.

Petley, Random Island.

Burgoyne's Cove's deep, sheltered coves have long supported a fishing industry. The slate cliffs inspired the Hurley Slate Works Company to open a facility. The town is named for British general John Burgoyne. In 1953, American brigadier general Richard Ellsworth crashed a Convair RB-36H Peacemaker bomber in Burgoyne's Cove on a trip from the Azores to South Dakota. A short hike leads up a hillside to the crash site, where debris is still visible.

Return 26 kilometres west on Route 232 to the intersection with Main Road. Turn right and ride northeast for 4 kilometres to Route 230, also known as the Bonavista Peninsula Highway or the Discovery Trail. Ride 14 kilometres to the exit onto Route 234, just past Lethbridge. Travelling

Jamestown.

north on Route 234 takes you up the side of Bonavista Bay.

As you ride north on Route 234, you quickly reach the left-hand exit into Brooklyn, which offers accommodations.

Return to Route 234 and ride 7 kilometres north to Portland, named for a white rock similar to one in Portland, England. Three kilometres from Portland is the community of Jamestown; then it's another 6 kilometres to Winter Brook at the end of Route 234. Quiet Winter Brook was once a thriving fishing, farming, logging, and trapping community. Some of these enterprises are still in production today, although on a smaller scale.

From Winter Brook, the direct return trip to Clarenville is 45 kilometres.

Trinity.
ELLISTON
238
PORT UNION
230
SOUTHERN BAY
PORT REXTON
CHAMPNEY'S WEST
239
GOOSE COVE
TRINITY
DUNFIELD
ENGLISH HARBOUR

Bonavista Peninsula, Discovery Trail

Southern Bay to Elliston

> Distance: **174 km**
>> Primary road(s): **Routes 230, 238, 239**
>>> Amenities: **Trinity, Port Rexton, Elliston**

This trip along the southern or Trinity Bay side of the Bonavista Peninsula starts and ends in the town of Southern Bay and follows Route 230 (Discovery Trail).

From Southern Bay, ride 21 kilometres along Route 230, then exit right onto Route 239 toward Trinity, Goose Cove, Dunfield, and Trouty. To ride through these communities and return to Route 230 is about 22 kilometres.

Three kilometres along Route 239 take a left-hand turn toward Trinity. For centuries, Trinity and its protected coves have been a hub for the fishing industry. Logging and shipbuilding also thrived there for the last three to four centuries. In the 21st century, tourism is the primary industry—a 2021 census recorded the population of Trinity as 76, a surprisingly low figure given the number of summer visitors. Consider attending a play performed by Rising Tide Theatre, which celebrates the culture and heritage of this historic community. This professional theatre company has been entertaining audiences in Newfoundland for over 40 years.

From Trinity, backtrack to the intersection with Route 239 and turn left. You next pass Goose Cove, home to Goose Cove Retreat; next is Dunfield (renamed from Cuckold's Cove in 1913), which boasts hiking trails and the historic Fort Point; and then scenic Trouty.

Return to Route 230, turn right and ride 3 kilometres to the Port Rexton Foodex, which has fuel, a grocery store, and

a liquor outlet. Adjacent to its parking lot is Rocky Hill Road, a 3-kilometre paved road into Trinity East, passing by Port Rexton Brewery, Gun Hill Lookout, accommodations, and the well-known Skerwink hiking trail.

Port Rexton (population 361) is part of Trinity Bight, which comprises 11 communities.

Return to Route 230 and ride eastward to the right-hand exit into Champney's West, where you can hike Fox Island Trail.

Back on Route 230, in 1 kilometre a right-hand exit leads to English Harbour. The English Harbour Arts Centre, housed in All Saints Anglican Church overlooking Trinity Bay, has hosted many artistic workshops and cultural events.

Continue northeast on Route 230 for 22 kilometres to Port Union. Built by William Coaker and the Fishermen's Protective Union, it is officially named the Port Union National Historic District of Canada for its history and architecture.

From Port Union, continue along Route 230 for another 18 kilometres to Elliston, the end point of this trip (we'll cover the town of Bonavista in Trip 35).

Elliston, originally called Bird Island Cove, was renamed in honour of Rev. William Ellis, the first Methodist missionary to this community. Elliston advertises itself as the root cellar

Champney's West.

Trinity Dock Marina Restaurant & Gallery was restored from a historic fishing premise.

Sealers Memorial statue, Elliston.

capital of the world (visit a tourist shop for a map of root cellars).

The SS *Southern Cross* and SS *Newfoundland* were involved in sealing disasters in 1914: 251 sealers froze to death. A statue erected in Elliston commemorates these men who lost their lives; the Sealer's Museum tells this history in detail.

Return to Southern Bay along Route 230—or continue on to Bonavista and Trip 25.

The Matthew Legacy building, Bonavista.

Bonavista Peninsula, Cabot Highway

Sweet Bay to Bonavista

> Distance: **207 km**
>> Primary road(s): **Route 235**
>>> Amenities: **Bonavista**

Sweet Bay is the starting point for this return trip along the northern shore of the Bonavista Peninsula on Route 235 (Bonavista Bay Highway or Cabot Highway). Sweet Bay was established as a fishing community in the early 1800s; its year-round population of 80 increases significantly in the summer.

From Sweet Bay, ride 10 kilometres to the intersection with Route 230 after 10 kilometres. Ride on Route 230 for 3 kilometres, then turn left into Southern Bay and onto Route 235. Ride 8 kilometres, then turn left into Summerville along Summerville Road.

In 2015, the population of Summerville was 39. This picturesque community has beautiful coastlines and houses and an operational fishing industry. At the end of Summerville is an abandoned house on top of a hill; from there, take a hiking trail to a viewpoint overlooking the coastline.

Return to Route 235, turn left, and ride 8 kilometres to Plate Cove West (population 174). This community is close to Plate Cove East, on the other side of the harbour. Plate Cove West has hiking trails, if you'd like to get off your bike. Round Da Bay Inn has a restaurant, art gallery, and a gift shop.

Continue 6 kilometres along Route 235, then turn left toward Open Hall, Red Cliff, and Tickle Cove. Open Hall and Red Cliff have been amalgamated as Open Hall-Red Cliff (population 60). Fishers from elsewhere in Newfoundland, including Greenspond, settled in this area in 1770, though

French fishers had settled here before this. Open Hall's harbour can accommodate small fishing boats.

Tickle Cove was used for the fishing scene in the 2013 Canadian movie *The Grand Seduction*. The most memorable feature of this area is Tickle Cove Sea Arch, composed of red sandstone and other conglomerates.

Head back onto Route 235 and travel 10 kilometres to King's Cove (population 75). A post office was established here

in 1851. Head northwest along Top Road for 5 kilometres to Duntara, and then take Main Road 4 kilometres to Keels, the location of a geological feature called "The Devil's Footprints."

Return to King's Cove and Route 235. Ride 4 kilometres to Knight's Cove, another fishing community that was settled in the late 1700s.

Continuing along Route 235, in 13 kilometres you can take the exit into Upper Amherst Cove (population 41), a

Plate Cove West.

fertile farming region and home to the Bonavista Social Club restaurant.

Return to Route 235 and ride 14 kilometres to Bonavista (population 3,190), the largest town on the peninsula. In 1497, Italian explorer John Cabot (Giovanni Caboto) landed in Bonavista and was impressed with the abundance of cod and seals. These fertile fishing grounds also attracted explorers from England, Spain, France, and Portugal.

The Ryan Premises in Bonavista, preserved as a national historic site and maintained by Parks Canada, is a restored fish merchant's fishing operation.

Seven kilometres north of the town of Bonavista is Cape Bonavista with its historic lighthouse, built in 1843. There's a puffin colony just beyond the lighthouse on a hilly island. Cape Bonavista is also an excellent place to look for whales and icebergs. Dungeon Provincial Park, with dramatic sea arches carved by the waves, is on the way to Cape Bonavista.

Return to Sweet Bay along Route 235 for a 207-kilometre day of exploring towns, coastlines, buildings, and tremendous beauty.

Tickle Cove sea arch.
Garrick Theatre, Bonavista.
Orange Hall, Bonavista.
Cape Bonavista Lighthouse.

North Harbour.

GOOBIES
SWIFT
CURRENT
NORTH
HARBOUR
GARDEN COVE
210
ENGLISH
HARBOUR
EAST
211
TERRENCEVILLE
HARBOUR MILLE
212
ST. BERNARD'S-JACQUES
FONTAINE

Goobies to Harbour Mille

> **Distance: 355 km**
>> **Primary road(s): Routes 210, 211, 212**
>>> **Amenities: Goobies, Swift Current**

Burin Peninsula: overview

Trips 36, 37, and 38 explore the Burin Peninsula, sometimes called "the boot" due to its geographical shape. Fisheries, mining, and shipbuilding have been the mainstays of the peninsula's economy. When I ride the peninsula, I allow two to four days to visit all of the communities.

Marystown, the largest centre, has a variety of hotels and restaurants and is usually where I overnight. Marystown has a population of about 5,000; it is 143 kilometres from the TCH on Route 210.

The Burin Peninsula is close to the French-owned islands of St. Pierre and Miquelon. From Fortune, take a 25-kilometre ferry ride to the only remaining French colonies in North America. If you have time to spend a day or two in France, you are definitely in for a treat.

Burin Peninsula North

Trip 36 covers the northern part of the Burin Peninsula, starting at the intersection of the TCH and Route 210 at Goobies. From there, we wander southward through a number of communities to Harbour Mille. If you return to Goobies, this ride is 355 kilometres, or you can connect it with Trips 37 and/or 38.

The exit to Route 210 (Burin Peninsula Highway or Heritage Run) from the TCH is well marked by an Irving Station with a large moose statue and a tourist information kiosk.

From Goobies, ride 12 kilometres south on Route 210 and take the left-hand exit to North Harbour. The community of North Harbour, about 7 kilometres south of Route 210, is on the Placentia Bay side of the Burin Peninsula.

Return to Route 210 and continue southwest for 10 kilometres to Swift Current. Stop at Vernon's Antique Toy Shop in Swift Current, home to a large collection of antique cars and trucks from 1908 to 1970 and one of the premier antique vehicle collections in North America.

Back on Route 210, continue 2 kilometres northwest to a left turn to Kilmory Resort. Its log chalets, built on treed lots overlooking waterways and hills, are popular year-round.

Ride 43 kilometres farther on Route 210 and take a right-

Harbour Mille.

hand exit onto Route 211. Three kilometres along Route 211, take the left-hand exit to picturesque Terrenceville (population 446), located in a valley at the head of Fortune Bay.

Return to Route 211, turn left, and ride about 30 kilometres southwest to the small community of English Harbour East, located on Belle Bay on the northern part of Fortune Bay.

From English Harbour, backtrack to Route 210. Ride 32 kilometres southwest and take a right-hand turn onto Route 212. The first community along this winding, paved road is St. Bernard's-Jacques Fontaine (population 433). Five kilometres farther is Bay L'Argent (population 234). From Bay L'Argent, take a ferry to Rencontre East, which is also accessible from Pool's Cove on the Connaigre Peninsula (see Trip 24).

Harbour Mille.
Little Harbour East.
Sandbar separating fresh and salt water, Terrenceville

From Bay L'Argent, it's a 15-kilometre coastal ride to Little Harbour East; the beach walk here is beautiful and a personal favourite. Three kilometres farther brings you to Harbour Mille (population 84) at the end of Route 212.

Wind your way back up the Burin Peninsula to Goobies for a 355-kilometre round trip.

Rushoon.
BOAT HARBOUR
PARKERS COVE
PETITE FORTE
SOUTH EAS[T]
BIGHT
BAINE HARBOUR
RED HARBOUR
210
SPANISH ROOM
MARYSTOWN
ROCK HARBOUR

Middle Burin Peninsula

Marystown to South East Bight plus Ferry

> Distance: **168 km**
>> Primary road(s): **Route 210**
>>> Amenities: **Marystown**

With about 5,000 residents, Marystown is the largest town on the Burin Peninsula and a vibrant centre with sporting events, museums, walking trails, fishing, and camping. Because of its deep harbour, Mortier Bay, just east of Marystown, has been used to repair ships and oil platforms. During World War II, Marystown was chosen by the British as the site to which the royal family could be evacuated if the Germans invaded England.

To start Trip 37, ride 7 kilometres north from Marystown on Route 210 (or the Heritage Run) to the right-hand exit to Spanish Room (population 131). Five kilometres past Spanish Room is Rock Harbour, a community of fewer than 100 people located on a beautiful protected harbour.

Backtrack to Route 210 and ride 13 kilometres north, then turn right at the Red Harbour exit. This fishing community was settled by former residents of Flat Island, just east of Red Harbour, during the 1960s resettlement program. Lobster, snow crab, and lumpfish roe are the primary products harvested here.

Return to Route 210 and ride north for 14 kilometres to the exit to the communities of Rushoon and Baine Harbour, which sit on two separate inlets in Placentia Bay.

Baine Harbour is nestled around another well-protected harbour looking out into Placentia Bay. It is an idyllic place to visit. Newfoundland artist Ed Roche has captured many Newfoundland communities; his oil painting of Baine Harbour

is a favourite of mine. See my photo (page 217) of the side of Baine Harbour that he painted.

Back on Route 210, ride approximately 1 kilometre north and exit right into the community of Parkers Cove.

Return to Route 210 and ride 4 kilometres to the exit toward Boat Harbour, Brookside (both on Boat Harbour), and Petite Forte. Boat Harbour (population 73) is home to Livyer's Lot Heritage Site, where you can enjoy local fare and crafts. From Boat Harbour, it's another 4 kilometres to Brookside and 23 to Petite Forte.

From Petite Forte, take a 25-minute ferry ride into South East Bight, 11 kilometres along the coastline of Placentia Bay. Visit 511nl.com for ferry schedules and information. Park your motorcycle in the designated lot and walk aboard the ferry. South East Bight (population <100) can be accessed only by ferry. The main source of transportation is ATV. In the 19th century, the community was a bustling place due to the fishing, farming, and a slate quarry.

After touring South East Bight and enjoying the return ferry trip, ride 66 kilometres from Petite Forte back to Marystown.

Ferry entering South East Bight.

Baine Harbour, where Ed Roche painted.

South East Bight.

Norcon Oceanus, Petite Forte.

Burin Bay Arm from Epworth.

Southern Burin Peninsula
"Bottom of the Boot"

> **Distance: 197 km**
>> **Primary road(s): Routes 213, 220, 221, 222**
>>> **Amenities: Burin, Fortune, Grand Bank**

Trip 38 loops around the bottom of the Burin Peninsula "boot," starting and finishing in Garnish and riding in a clockwise direction. You'll enjoy hours of riding beside the ocean and the chance to check out more than a dozen communities with fascinating maritime history.

Most of this ride is on Route 220, though we start in Garnish, on Route 213, a diversion off Route 220. Garnish (population 542) was known for its lumber industry; these days, it's better known for lobster. Garnish is protected from the ocean by a long sandbar; and a 150-year-old lighthouse stands at the entrance to town. Its harbour is also fed by Garnish River, a fertile salmon river.

From Garnish, ride southeast for 5 kilometres on Route 213 and turn southeast on Route 222. Ride 15 kilometres, circumventing Marystown. At the end of Route 222, turn onto Route 221 toward Burin, which has been populated for more than 300 years, and as of 2021 has over 2,200 residents (including those of nearby Burin Bay Arm, Bulls Cove, Ship Cove, Collins Cove, and others).

A few metres from the Burin Heritage House on the road into Burin is the Burin Bay Arm boardwalk overlooking the bay. Like many Newfoundland communities, Burin suffered greatly in the wake of the cod moratorium of 1992. The town's fish plant, run by High Liner Foods, closed in 2012—but reopened by Oceanic Releaf in 2021 as a cannabis processing facility.

Fortune.

From Burin, continue 5 kilometres along Route 221 to Bulls Cove. Near Bulls Cove is Smugglers Cove Roadhouse, a pub and grill and home to the Heritage Riders motorcycle group, which organizes an annual fundraising ride from Goobies on the TCH to the roadhouse. This 163-kilometre "Ride the Boot" attracts hundreds of bikers and raises money for autism programs on the peninsula.

After a meal at Smugglers Cove, continue northeast for 2 kilometres to Port au Bras. On November 18, 1929, a tsunami struck the Burin Peninsula, killing 27 people in seven communities and washing some communities out to sea. In Port au Bras, at the head of the bay, a memorial park and statue commemorate the 27 lives lost.

Fox Cove and Mortier are 4 kilometres northeast of Port au Bras. In Mortier, visit Hartson's Lookout, a small museum sitting on the coastline.

Port au Bras tsunami commemorative statue.

The view from Point May.

After this diversion along Route 221, return to the intersection of Routes 221 and 220 and turn left at Burin Bay Arm. Ride 10 kilometres to Epworth, where you can look back over the hills to see the boardwalk you just left in Burin Bay Arm. Continue along Route 220 to Little St. Lawrence, the location of a Newfoundland and Labrador Hydro-owned generating station.

Three kilometres west of Little St. Lawrence is St. Lawrence (population 1,115). Traditionally, fishing was the mainstay of this community; starting in the 1930s, the American Newfoundland Fluorspar Company mined for about 40 years in the area, leaving a heartbreaking legacy of industrial disease. In the 2000s, the provincial government installed nine wind turbines in the St. Lawrence area.

From St. Lawrence, continue in a clockwise route around the boot for 14 kilometres to Lawn (population 583). This town,

wrapped around a small harbour, has survived off the plentiful fishing grounds on its coastline. Three islands visible offshore are part of the Lawn Bay Ecological Reserve.

The coastline between Lawn and St. Lawrence was the site of the sinking of the USS *Truxtun* and USS *Pollux*, which were grounded in a storm in 1942. Residents of St. Lawrence and Lawn were critical in the rescue efforts; 185 sailors survived the wrecks, 203 perished.

Continue along Route 220, passing through the communities of Lamaline, Allan's Island, High Beach, Calmer, and Point May. On a clear day you can see the French islands of St. Pierre and Miquelon. From Point May, continue 22 kilometres to the town of Fortune, the departure point of the St. Pierre and Miquelon ferries. You can take your car or motorcycle to the French islands on the one-hour ferry trip (check schedule and availability: www.spm-ferries.fr/en/).

Fortune (population 1,285) gets its name from the Portuguese *fortuna*, meaning "harbour of good fortune."

From Fortune, it is 7 kilometres to Grand Bank (population 2,580). This community, settled by French fishers, who called it *Grand Banc*, is a profitable fishing hub because of its ice-free harbour and plentiful fishing grounds.

From Grand Bank, continue for 22 kilometres along the coast to Grand Beach (population 65). Another 10 kilometres brings you to the left-hand exit onto Route 213 through Frenchman's Cove Provincial Park on your way back into Garnish. This park is a beautiful habitat of pebble beaches, marshes, and streams; it is also home to the 9-hole Grande Meadows Golf Club.

Just 8 kilometres north of Frenchman's Cove, you end your journey in Garnish.

Little St. Lawrence hydro facility.

Garnish.

Grand Bank fish plant.

Private floating wharf, Mount Arlington Heights.

SUNNYSIDE
COME BY CHANCE
ARNOLD'S COVE
TCH
CHANCE COVE
BELLEVUE
NORMAN'S COVE-LONG COVE
201
202
CHAPEL ARM
LONG HARBOUR-MOUNT ARLINGTON HEIGHTS

③⑨ Isthmus of Avalon

> › Distance: **162 km**
> ›› Primary road(s): **TCH; Routes 201, 202**
> ››› Amenities: **Arnold's Cove, Sunnyside**

The Avalon Peninsula is attached to the rest of the island of Newfoundland by a 6-kilometre-wide isthmus between Placentia and Trinity Bays. On this isthmus, you meet fog on most summer days, but it dissipates quickly.

Riding the TCH southeast from Goobies, you enter the isthmus of Avalon with Sunnyside in Trinity Bay on the left and Come By Chance in Placentia Bay on the right.

Trip 39 starts in Sunnyside (population 407), a community stretching 5 kilometres along Bull Arm. A transatlantic telegraph cable was laid in Sunnyside in 1858. Queen Victoria of England and President James Buchanan of the US communicated over this cable. Explorer John Guy met the Beothuks of this region in 1612 and named the area Truce Sound.

Besides being loggers and fishers, the people of Sunnyside became workers at the oil refinery across the isthmus in Come By Chance, and at the Hibernia Oil Platform, which was partially built in Bull Arm.

From Sunnyside, cross under the TCH and ride toward Placentia Bay along Main Road, where you arrive at the former Come By Chance oil refinery. In 2024, the oil refinery reopened as a producer of biofuels after an extensive refit by Braya Renewable Fuels. Come By Chance is a small community near the refinery. If you're looking to stretch your legs, try the hike along the Come By Chance River valley.

From Come By Chance, continue along Main Road to

Stone moose, Bellevue area.

Chance Cove.

Arnold's Cove. The anchor and chain displayed beside the TCH at the entrance to Arnold's Cove belonged to the MT *Ardtaraig*, which broke away when at anchor in Bar Haven in Placentia Bay in 1976. The vessel was forced to return to sea; the anchor and chain were retrieved from the ocean floor in 2003 and are displayed in Herb Brett Memorial Park.

The prosperous fishing community of Arnold's Cove (population 964) boasts lookouts over Placentia Bay as well as Big Pond Bird Sanctuary. Drake House in Arnold's Cove, built in 1890 and designated a heritage structure by the Heritage Foundation of Newfoundland and Labrador in 2003, now houses a community museum.

Return to the TCH at the Come By Chance exit, ride south on the TCH for 21 kilometres, and turn left toward the community of Chance Cove. You are now on the Trinity Bay side of the TCH. From Chance Cove (population 213) are spectacular views of the coastline and Trinity Bay. If you have an hour or

two, from the beach in Chance Cove walk the Coastal Hiking Trail, which leads to uphill walking trails alongside hidden beaches, lookouts, and caves.

From Chance Cove, ride in a southeasterly direction around Tickle Bay, passing through the communities of Bellevue Beach and Bellevue. Bellevue Beach campground offers ocean- and lakeside camping.

From Bellevue Beach, continue on Route 201 for 14 kilometres to Norman's Cove-Long Cove (population 647). This town and surrounding area boast hiking trails which showcase this part of Trinity Bay.

Ride 6 kilometres south on Route 201 to Chapel Arm, which has a large breakwater with docking facilities.

Ride southwest from Chapel Arm along Route 201 and go under the TCH onto Route 202 over to Long Harbour-Mount Arlington Heights. We have now gone from Trinity Bay back to Placentia Bay. Long Harbour-Mount Arlington Heights is best known for the Long Harbour Nickel Processing Plant.

Head north on the TCH to Sunnyside to make this a 162-kilometre round trip.

Castle Hill, Placentia.

WHITBOURNE
TCH
100
PLACENTIA
COLINET
90
MT. CARMEL-MITCHELLS
BROOK-ST. CATHERINES
GOOSEBERRY COVE
PROVINCIAL PARK
SHIP COVE
92
ST. BRIDE'S
BRANCH
CAPE ST. MARY'S
ECOLOGICAL
RESERVE

 # Whitbourne to Cape St. Mary's

> Distance: **281 km**
>> Primary road(s): **TCH; Routes 90, 92, 100**
>>> Amenities: **Whitbourne, Placentia**

Whitbourne, Newfoundland's first inland town, is named for an early settler, Sir Richard Whitbourne, who was governor of Renews from 1680 to 1720. The town of Whitbourne was founded more than two centuries later, in 1880, as the railway was being built. Sir Robert Bond, premier of the Newfoundland colony and prime minister of the Dominion of Newfoundland from 1900 to 1909, was instrumental to the development of the town and lived there as well.

Whitbourne (population 955) is today a regional service centre and also home to the Wetlands Conservation Trail.

Trip 40 begins at the Whitbourne Irving on the TCH or the tourist information centre at the same parking lot, about 5 kilometres north of the town of Whitbourne.

From the parking lot, head south on Route 100 toward Placentia. In about 35 kilometres is Dunville, where in 2007 tropical storm Chantal significantly damaged the town's road structure.

En route from Dunville to Placentia (8 kilometres away), take a right-hand turn to Argentia, home to a former American naval base as well as the Argentia ferry terminal. Vessels leaving this terminal, which opened in 1967, carry passengers and vehicles to North Sydney, Nova Scotia, with a sailing time of between 14 and 19 hours.

Heading back toward Route 100 and Placentia, you pass Freshwater, which overlooks Red Island about 12 kilometres

Cape St. Mary's Ecological Reserve Interpretive Centre.

Cape St. Mary's Ecological Reserve.

Gooseberry Cove Park.

northwest of Placentia in Placentia Bay. Residents of Red Island left in 1968 during the provincial resettlement program, though many summer homes and cabins remain on the island.

Before reaching Placentia, you can take a right-hand exit to Castle Hill National Historic Site, a stone fortress overlooking Placentia. Walk the trails around the remnants of French and British fortifications and military weapons.

Closer to the town of Placentia is Jerseyside, connected to Placentia by the Sir Ambrose Lift Bridge.

Placentia Bay was home to Beothuks in the 1500s for two centuries and later the Mi'kmaq were here. English and French fishers and settlers arrived by the late 17th century. Basque fishers also used this part of the New World. By 1655, the French controlled half of Newfoundland and their capital was Placentia (Plaisance). The area's colourful history is well preserved in Placentia's tourist office and historical buildings, as well as the Castle Hill National Historic Site.

Head southwest from Placentia on Route 210 for 23 kilometres to Ship Cove on the west side of Placentia Bay. Four kilometres south of Ship Cove is the community of Gooseberry

Crossing into Placentia.

Branch.

Sacred Heart Catholic Church, St. Bride's.

Cove; its park and beach are referred to as the Jewel of the Cape Shore Highway. Gooseberry Cove is an ideal stop for hiking, swimming, sunbathing, and picnicking.

Five kilometres south of Gooseberry Cove Park is the Patrick's Cove-Angels Cove local service district (population 56), a traditional fishing and farming area. Patrick's Cove was once known as Devil's Cove.

Just 10 kilometres south is the town of St. Bride's. This fishing community had 318 people in the 2021 census. St. Bride's is home to Sacred Heart Catholic Church.

East on Route 100, within 4 kilometres, is a right-hand turn to Cape St. Mary's Ecological Reserve, known as "the Cape," a magnificent place to see thousands of nesting gannets, kittiwakes, and other species of seabirds. You can appreciate these birds from as close as 10 metres as you stand on the cliffs. You will have to leave your bike and hike 1 kilometre to see this amazing site. An interpretation centre is located at the start of the hike to the nesting bird cliffs.

Return to Route 100 and ride 14 kilometres to Branch (population 177) on St. Mary's Bay on the eastern side of this peninsula. Irish settlers were in this area in the 1700s. Continue 56 kilometres to Colinet; this is a serene motorcycle ride with long winding roads and vast vistas of marshes and grasslands.

From Colinet on Route 91, head east to Mount Carmel and then ride 24 kilometres to the TCH (take the route to avoid 13 kilometres of gravel road straight north of Colinet).

Back on the TCH, you will soon reach the Irving station where you started this trip 281 kilometres ago.

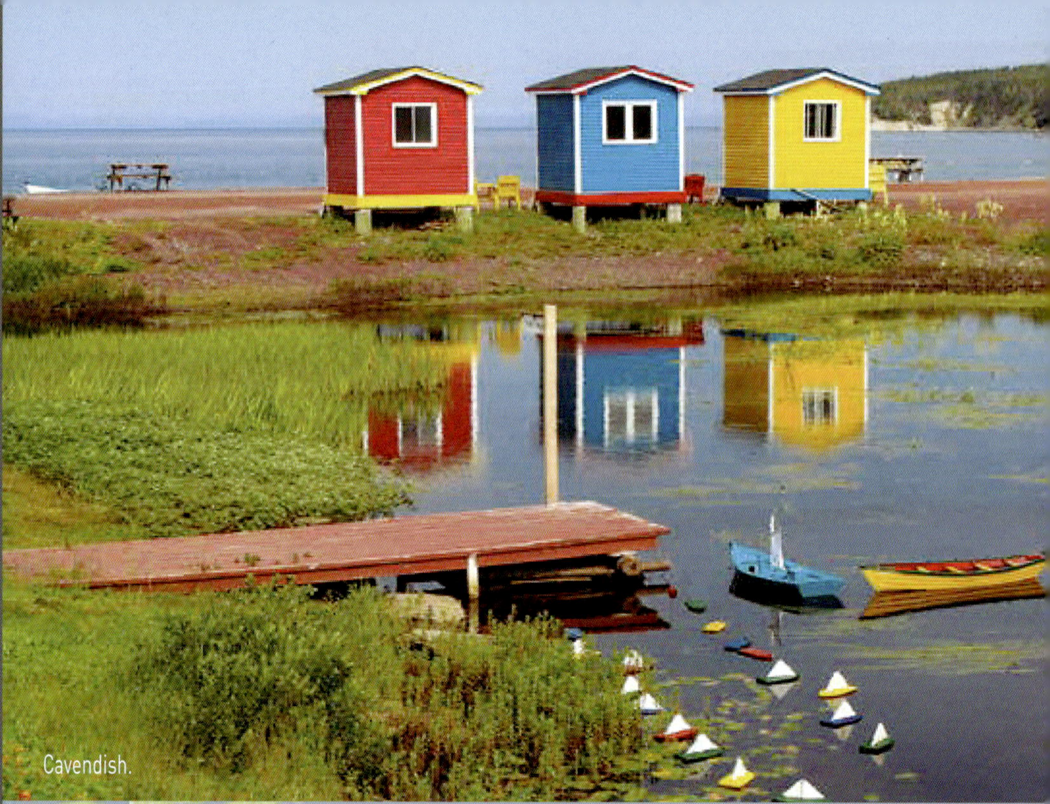

Cavendish.

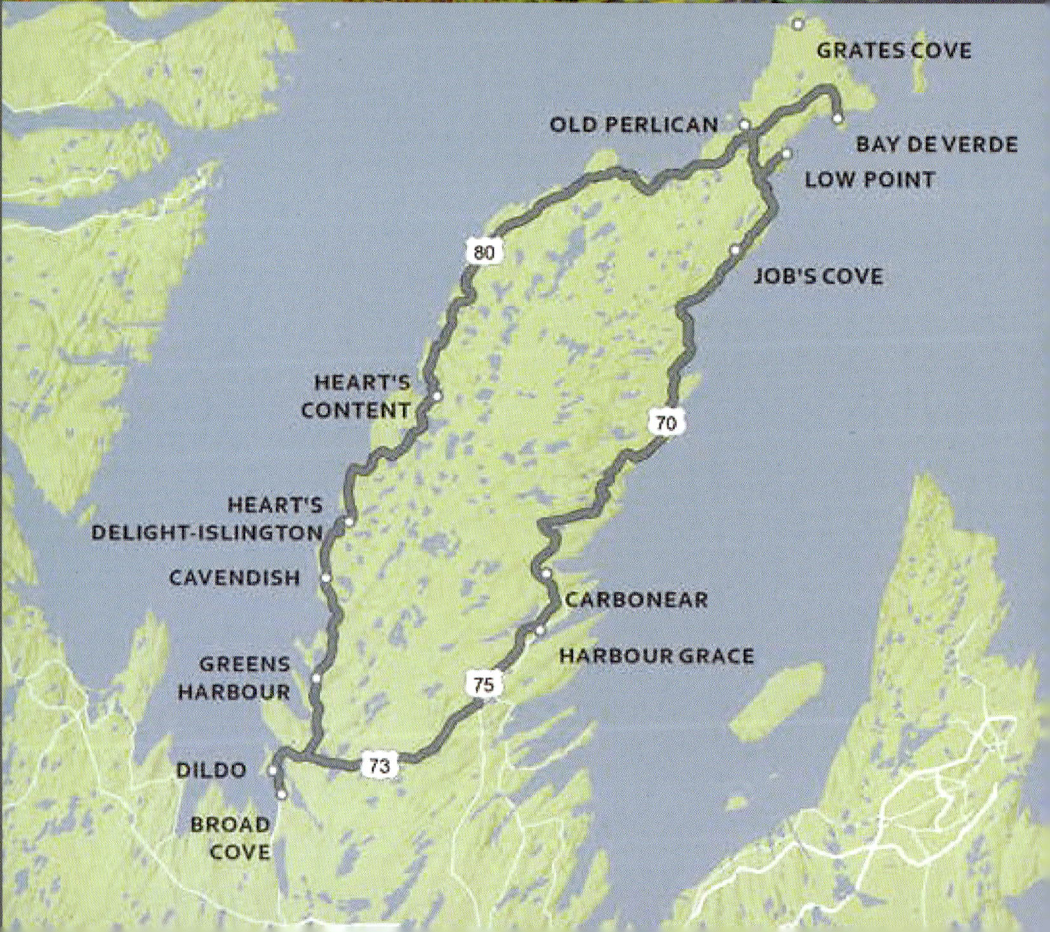
GRATES COVE
OLD PERLICAN
BAY DE VERDE
LOW POINT
80
JOB'S COVE
HEART'S CONTENT
70
HEART'S DELIGHT-ISLINGTON
CAVENDISH
CARBONEAR
HARBOUR GRACE
GREENS HARBOUR
75
73
DILDO
BROAD COVE

④ Dildo to Grates Cove

> Distance: **229 km**
>> Primary road(s): **Routes 70, 73, 75, 80**
>>> Amenities: **Dildo, Bay de Verde, Carbonear**

Dildo and South Dildo are both located on Dildo Arm on southeastern Trinity Bay. South Dildo has about 200 residents; Dildo, 800. This area was populated by Maritime Archaic people in 2000 BCE and about 2,700 years later by Dorset and later again by Beothuk, likely attracted by abundant cod, whale, and seal.

In 2019, American TV personality Jimmy Kimmel and his sidekick Guillermo Rodriquez were made honorary mayor and citizen of Dildo. A Hollywood-style DILDO sign on the hillside overlooking the town was gifted as a friendly gesture from the Jimmy Kimmel Show. The Dildo Brewing Company and Museum, on the Dildo waterfront, serves its own beer and a wide selection of food. A few hundred metres away, the Dildo Dory Grill serves Newfoundland cuisine.

From Dildo along the eastern side of Trinity Bay and around Conception Bay to St. John's is known as the Baccalieu Trail.

Ride 12 kilometres north of Dildo to the oceanfront town of Green's Harbour; 7 kilometres farther is Whiteway (population 351). Often on summer days, you'll see tour boats sailing to the rock formations called Shag Rock in the middle of the cove. Passengers are entertained by cormorants, large diving birds known locally as "shags."

The next community, Cavendish (population 301), boasts a colourful display of small sheds and stages on its beach.

Seven kilometres north of Cavendish, still on Route 80, is

Heart's Delight-Islington (population 646). Continue riding to the communities of Heart's Desire and Heart's Content. Heart's Content was the site of the first transatlantic telegraph cable to North America. In 1866, Heart's Content Cable Station became the western terminus of the North Atlantic telegraph cable; the eastern terminus was on Valentia Island in Ireland. This cable was used until 1965 and the station was designated a provincial historic site in 1974.

Continue north from Heart's Content along Route 80 for 46 kilometres to Old Perlican. Along the way, you pass New Perlican, Turk's Cove, Winterton (home of the Wooden Boat Museum of Newfoundland and Labrador), Hant's Harbour, New Chelsea, New Melbourne, Brownsdale, and Sibley's Cove.

Shag Rock, Whiteway.

The historic fishing community of Old Perlican was visited by English fishers starting in the 17th century. Visit the Old Perlican Harbour Authority, Beckett Heritage Property, or local walking trails.

From Old Perlican, continue north to Grates Cove at the northernmost tip of the Bay de Verde Peninsula. Grates Cove, settled in 1790, is today known for its acres of rock walls; "The Walled Landscape of Grates Cove," designated a national historic site of Canada in 1995, is worth exploring.

Leave Grates Cove on Route 70 south and head along the eastern side of the peninsula. Consider taking the left-hand exits off Route 70 south of Grates Cove to Red Head Cove,

Stone Jug Restaurant and Bar, Carbonear.
Salmon Cove Sands.
Heart's Content.
BETWEEN ENGLAND AND THE CONTINENT

St. Peter's Catholic Church (ca. 1891), Carbonear.

Bay de Verde, and Low Point and experience the rugged, hilly coastline. Reduce your speed as you enter these communities—the roads are quite steep.

The landscape around Bay de Verde (population 347) is barren, but it has been a booming fishing community since the 1600s.

Return to Route 70 and ride south along Conception Bay. Over the next 45 kilometres, you pass through a dozen or so small communities before reaching Broad Cove. Broad Cove boasts a 1.6-kilometre out-and-back trail which takes about 20 minutes to complete.

Continue south to Kingston and then Salmon Cove (population 764) and Salmon Cove Sands, a heart-shaped sandy beach surrounded by cliffs. Dismount for a beach stroll, a hike on the 2-kilometre trail, or to grab a snack from the canteen.

Before leaving the Conception Bay coastline, ride 13 kilometres south to Carbonear. This town of nearly 5,000 people has been tied to fishing and shipbuilding throughout its history. It is one of the oldest European settlements in North America and has been included on Portuguese maps dating to the late 1500s.

Ride southwest from Carbonear on Route 70 to Route 75 to Tilton. Turn onto Route 73 (New Harbour Barrens) and ride to New Harbour in Trinity Bay and back to Dildo.

Mermaid statues, Bay Bulls harbour.
13
BAY BULLS
WITLESS BAY
TORS COVE
MOUNT CARMEL
CAPE BROYLE
90
RIVERHEAD
FERRYLAND
AQUAFORTE
ST. MARY'S
RENEWS
HOLYROOD POND
ST. VINCENT'S
10
TREPASSEY
PORTUGAL
COVE SOUTH

42 The Irish Loop

The Irish Loop starts south of St. John's, at Bay Bulls. From Bay Bulls to St. Vincent's, the Irish Loop is Route 10; at Holyrood Pond, it becomes Route 90 (Salmonier Line) and heads northeast to the TCH and then east back to Bay Bulls. The Irish Loop winds around the Avalon Wilderness Reserve, 1,070 square kilometres of forests, bogs, and barrens. As there is much to see along these 268 kilometres of road, plan a full day for this trip.

Bay Bulls (population 1,566) is on a sheltered bay south of St. John's. The community has appeared on maps dating to the late 1500s, attractive for its relative proximity to the rich fishing area of the Grand Banks. In the 21st century, Bay Bulls is also a service hub for offshore oil and gas operations. Two popular bird and whale boat tours operate out of Bay Bulls, bringing guests close to whales, puffins, and other sea life.

From Bay Bulls, ride 5 kilometres south on Route 10 to Witless Bay (population 1,640). The four small islands of the Witless Bay Ecological Reserve are home to one of the largest puffin colonies (up to 260,000 breeding pairs) in North America. Other seabird species, including storm petrels and kittiwakes, also make their summer homes on these islands.

Eight kilometres farther south along Route 10 is picturesque Tors Cove (formerly Toads Cove, population 300). The next community is Cape Broyle (population 499), with strong Irish connections dating to the 1780s. As of 2024,

Tors Cove.

Cape Broyle's fish processing plant is still operational. The community is a popular starting point for kayaking tours and East Coast Trail hikes.

At Ferryland, 12 kilometres farther along Route 10, visit the Colony of Avalon, established in 1621 by Sir George Calvert, the first Lord Baltimore. Because of decades of archaeological work, this early English settlement is one of the best-preserved colonial sites in Newfoundland, with restored buildings and cobblestone streets. The Colony of Avalon was named a national historic site of Canada in 1953; the Historic Ferryland Museum was designated a municipal heritage site in 2006.

Approximately 5 kilometres south of Ferryland is the fishing community of Aquaforte (population 74); 13 kilometres later, Renews and Cappahayden.

From here, the road can be desolate, but it's a peaceful ride (unless you encounter wind across these barrens). Watch for caribou. At Portugal Cove South (population 86), check out the Edge of Avalon Interpretation Centre, from which you

can take a tour to see the fossils of Mistaken Point, a UNESCO World Heritage Site.

Ride another 11 kilometres to Trepassey, the approximate halfway point of the Irish Loop and Amelia Earhart's departure point as she left to become the first woman to fly the Atlantic Ocean as a passenger in 1928. Trepassey was a prosperous fishing community for centuries, until the cod fishery collapsed in 1992.

Continue west from Trepassey across the barrens for 31 kilometres to St. Vincent's-St. Stephen's-Peter's River. St. Vincent's Beach cuts across Holyrood Pond; the bridge at the end of pond stretches across "The Gut," which separates Holyrood Pond from the Atlantic Ocean. In June and July, pause at St. Vincent's Beach to look for whales; it's a frequent feeding ground for humpback whales.

This coastline is prone to fog. Some days may start out with spectacular sunshine and later may turn foggy. This should be no reason to stop you—the bike riding is fabulous

Antique auto, St. Mary's.

on these coasts of the Avalon Peninsula. Departing from St. Vincent's-St. Stephen's-Peter's River, you will be travelling on Route 90, the west side of the Irish Loop; in 16 kilometres, you reach St. Mary's.

Point La Haye Beach, just south of St. Mary's, is a nice place to stop for a picnic lunch. St. Mary's Bay Fisheries, which has held processing licences for groundfish, whelk, and snow crab, is a main employer in the area.

Ride north along St. Mary's Harbour for 10 kilometres to Riverhead. The next stretch of road travels along Salmonier Arm to St. Catherine's (Mount Carmel-Mitchells Brook-St. Catherine's, population 382). At St. Catherine's, you are at the top eastern side of Salmonier Arm; across the water is Mount Carmel.

About 24 kilometres farther along Route 90 (Salmonier Line), you reach the TCH. En route, you pass the Wilds Resort and Golf Course as well as the Salmonier Nature Park.

On the TCH, ride 12 kilometres north, then turn right onto Route 13 (Witless Bay Line) to return to Bay Bulls.

From Bay Bulls around the Irish Loop back to Bay Bulls is 268 kilometres, with some of best sights on the eastern side of Newfoundland and, for that matter, Canada.

View from St. Catherine's across Salmonier Arm.

Aquaforte.

St. Stephen's.

245

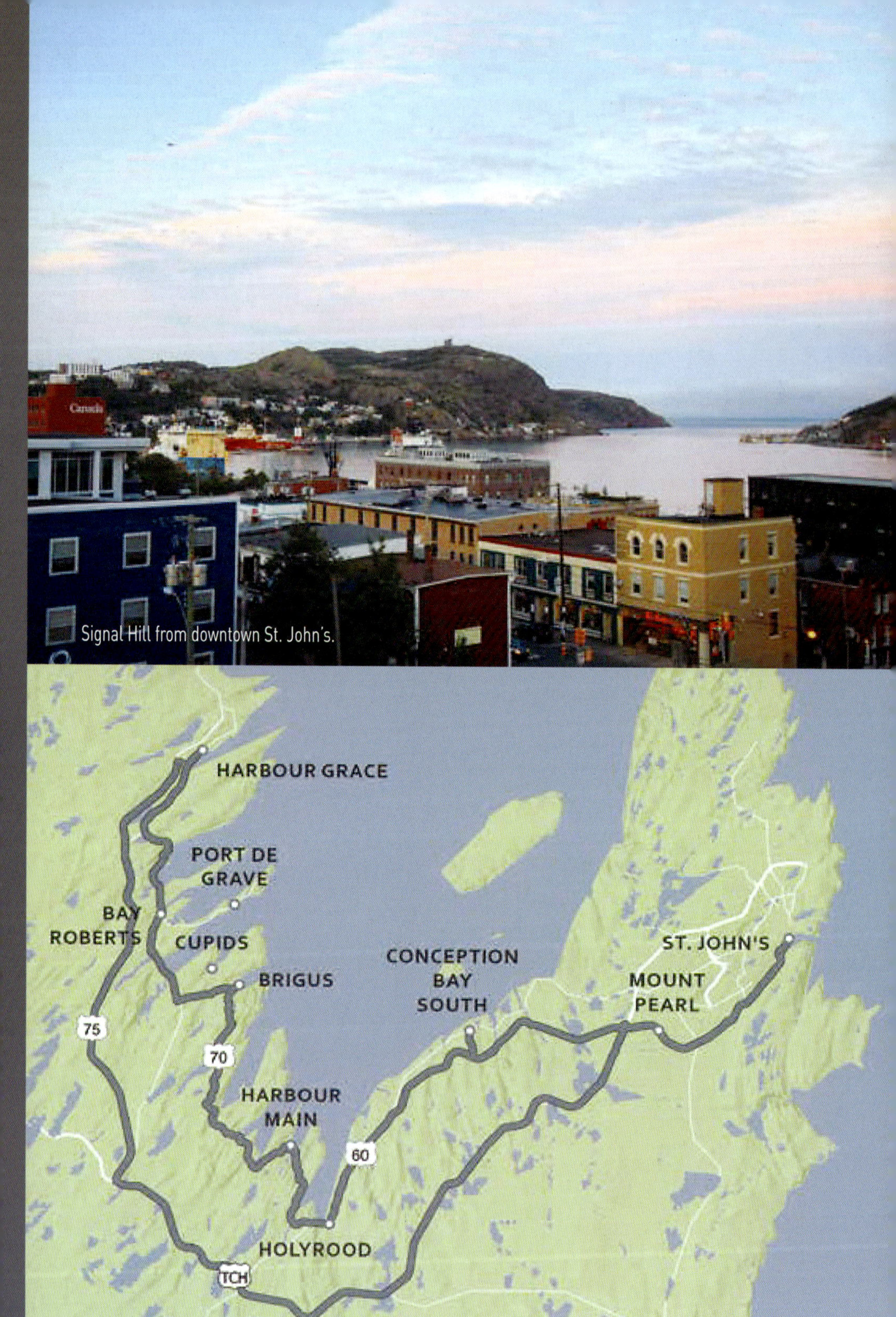

Signal Hill from downtown St. John's.
HARBOUR GRACE
PORT DE
GRAVE
BAY
ROBERTS
CUPIDS
BRIGUS
CONCEPTION
BAY
SOUTH
ST. JOHN'S
MOUNT
PEARL
75
70
HARBOUR
MAIN
60
HOLYROOD
TCH

Conception Bay

Harbour Grace to St. John's

> Distance: **233 km**
>> Primary road(s): **TCH; Routes 60, 70, 75**
>>> Amenities: **Frequent**

Trip 43 takes you from Harbour Grace in Conception Bay southeast to St. John's, the capital of Newfoundland and Labrador. The road along the Conception Bay coast is slow-going but the towns are worth taking time to see. The return route from St. John's is directly along the TCH.

Trip overview: first, ride south from Harbour Grace on Route 70 to Cupids. Next take Route 60 (Conception Bay Highway) to Mount Pearl, where Route 60 becomes Topsail Road and takes you into St. John's. From St. John's, return to Harbour Grace via the TCH and Route 75.

Now let's get into some detail.

Harbour Grace (population 2,796), founded by King Francis of France in 1517, is one of the oldest towns in North America. The pirate Peter Easton built a fort in Harbour Grace in 1610 and made the town his headquarters. England set up a neighbouring community in Bristol's Hope. Through the 1920s and 1930s, aviation pioneers, including Amelia Earhart, began using Harbour Grace as a place to begin transatlantic flights. The Royal Canadian Navy used it as a port of call during World War II and built a wireless station on the Harbour Grace airfield to monitor for German U-boats.

To learn more about this town and its heritage, visit the Conception Bay Museum, the Municipal Heritage Building, or the Gordon G. Pike Railway Heritage Museum.

From Harbour Grace, proceed south along Route 70 for 8

kilometres to Spaniard's Bay (population 2,630), named for the Basque and Portuguese fishers who plied their trade there in the 16th and 17th centuries. Throughout Spaniard's Bay history, salt, rum, and tobacco were traded for cod.

Ride another 8 kilometres south on Route 70 (Conception Bay Highway) to Bay Roberts, a modern town of 6,012. Bay Roberts is a transportation and distribution hub because it is a year-round shipping port with access to the population of the Avalon Peninsula.

In the 16th century, Bay Roberts was visited by English, French, Portuguese, and Spanish fishers. It was also renowned for barrel making and shipbuilding ventures.

In 1909, a printing plant in Bay Roberts published a weekly newspaper, *The Guardian*. Later, the Western Union Cable Company out of New York opened the Atlantic Cable Relay Station. The cable building is today a provincial heritage structure, a national historic site, and home to the Road to Yesterday Museum and the Christopher Pratt Art Gallery.

Take Route 72 east of Bay Roberts and ride 6 kilometres to the Port de Grave Peninsula. The peninsula's communities include Black Duck Pond, Bareneed, Port de Grave, Ship Cove, Blow Me Down, Hibb's Hole, Pick Eyes, Hussey's Cove, and Otterbury, with a combined population of 975.

Return from the Port de Grave Peninsula and head south on Route 70, then turn left onto Route 60 toward Cupids (population 699).

Cupids, established by English explorer John Guy in 1610, is the oldest continuously settled British colony in Canada. In 2010, the Cupids Legacy Centre was built to celebrate the community's 400th anniversary.

Five kilometres south of Cupids on Route 60 is the town of Brigus. A tunnel bored through solid rock on the Brigus waterfront provided access to a deepwater bay for sailing ships in 1860.

You stay close to the waters of Conception Bay as you ride Route 60 south from Brigus.

Conception Harbour (population 624), 13 kilometres

Cupids.
SS *Kyle* ran aground in Harbour Grace in 1967.
Brigus.
Conception Harbour.

Spaniards Room heritage home, Spaniard's Bay.

Conception Bay Museum, Harbour Grace.

south of Brigus, includes the former communities of Bacon Cove, Cat's Cove, Kitchuses, and Silver Spring. Next you pass through Avondale, Harbour Main-Chapel Cove-Lakeview, and Holyrood (considered the "bottom of the bay"). Holyrood is known for its oil refinery, its rolling caplin in late spring, its beautiful boardwalk and beach, and the annual Squid Fest.

Continue northeast on Route 60 through Conception Bay South (CBS), the second largest settlement in Newfoundland and Labrador (population 27,168). CBS is the amalgamation of Seal Cove, Lawrence Pond, Upper Gullies, Kelligrews, Foxtrap, Long Pond, Manuels, Chamberlains, and Topsail. The Kelligrews Soiree Folk Festival and Garden Party is a major summer event—stop by if you can.

Stay on Route 60 through Mount Pearl (the city adjacent to St. John's); the road becomes Topsail Road and eventually leads to Water Street in downtown St. John's. Just so you know you are on track, a motorcycle shop called Honda One is on your right-hand side in Mount Pearl on Topsail Road.

There's plenty to do in St. John's (population 111,914); see Trip 44.

For today, backtrack about 18 kilometres on Topsail Road through Mount Pearl until you reach the TCH overpass. Get on the TCH heading west and ride 55 kilometres to a right-hand exit onto Route 70, which shortly turns into Route 75 (Veteran's Memorial Highway). Stay on Route 75 for about 40 kilometres to the exit to Harbour Grace.

Port de Grave.

Saw about a dozen and a half bikers pull into a gas station. After watching them stop at the pumps, start up their bikes and ride to the front of the convenience store, stop, then fire up their bikes again and take off, I've come to conclusion that the most time consuming activity bikers engage in is finding neutral.

—Foster Kinn, *Freedom's Rush II: More Tales from the Biker and the Beast*

St. John's Harbour from Signal Hill.

The Battery.

POUCH COVE
20
BAULINE
FLATROCK
21
LOGY BAY-MIDDLE
COVE-OUTER COVE
40
30
BELL ISLAND
PORTUGAL
COVE
ST. JOHN'S
CAPE SPEAR
11
TCH
PETTY
HARBOUR-MADDOX COVE

㊹ Northeast Avalon

Petty Harbour to Bell Island to Petty Harbour

> Distance: **147 km**
>> Primary road(s): **Routes 11, 20, 21, 30, 40**
>>> Amenities: **Frequent**

This trip starts in Petty Harbour-Maddox Cove (population 947), about 16 kilometres south of St. John's. This area, settled since 1598, is one of the oldest settlements in North America. The name Petty Harbour comes from the French *Petit Havre*, meaning small harbour.

Fishing is a major source of income for residents. Any day during the summer you'll see fishers bringing in their daily catches. The town's hydroelectric generating station was the first in the province.

The Petty Harbour Mini Aquarium has touch tanks, live animal displays, and daily visitor programs. Other attractions include North Atlantic Ziplines, the Petty Harbour-Maddox Cove Heritage Museum, and the East Coast Trail. The narrow streets make this town a delight to ride on motorcycle.

Begin the trip just west of Petty Harbour-Maddox Cove on Crocker's Bridge on Petty Harbour Road between Second and First Ponds. Ride north on Route 11. After approximately 5 kilometres, you reach an intersection; turn right and ride east. After about 4 kilometres is Blackhead, which has a small museum in a restored one-room schoolhouse. Ride another 3 kilometres to Cape Spear Lighthouse National Historic Site, the most easterly point in North America. It is the first, and possibly best, place to watch the sunrise on the continent. Walk the trails and watch for icebergs, whales, and seabirds.

Backtrack along Route 11 past Blackhead, but instead of

Cabot Tower.

turning toward Petty Harbour, stay right on Blackhead Road, heading into St. John's. At the first set of lights, turn right onto Water Street through downtown St. John's and onto Signal Hill Road. Ride to the top to the Signal Hill National Historic Site, where Guglielmo Marconi received the first transatlantic wireless signal on December 12, 1901. In the summer, catch the Signal Hill Tattoo, a historical animation program portraying the life of the Newfoundland Regiment and the 27th Company 2nd Battalion-Royal Regiment from the 1790s.

St. John's is the most easterly city in continental North America and one of the oldest. The Venetian explorer John Cabot came to this harbour on June 24, 1497. There is much to do and see here, from arts and culture to fine restaurants and shopping to parks and recreation activities. If you have time, take a boat tour leaving from St. John's Harbour, which will take you along the stunning coastline.

Ride back down Signal Hill Road and take a right turn onto Empire Avenue, then right again onto King's Bridge Road and a left onto New Cove Road. Stay on New Cove Road until you hit Portugal Cove Road, which brings you to the town of Portugal Cove-St. Phillips (population 8,415). It's about 17 kilometres

Cape Spear Lighthouse.

Commemorating Pope John Paul II's 1987 visit to Flatrock.

Pouch Cove slipway.

from Signal Hill to the ferry terminal in Portugal Cove. From here, take the ferry to Bell Island in Conception Bay.

This ferry run generally has a two-boat schedule and the 20-minute crossings for cars, motorcycles, and pedestrians occur about every hour from 6 a.m. to 9 p.m. For the most up-to-date times and prices, visit 511nl.com.

Bell Island, which is about 9.7 kilometres long and 3.5 kilometres wide, was once home to prosperous underground iron ore mines (the Bell Island Mine Tour is excellent; visit bellislandminetour.com for information). Drilling below Conception Bay began in the 1890s and the ore was shipped to Nova Scotia to be smelted.

During World War II, two German U-boats attacked four iron ore ships moored near Bell Island in September and November of 1945 and 70 sailors lost their lives. As well, the iron ore loading dock was struck by a torpedo. This was one of the few direct attacks on North America in the war. A war memorial was constructed in Lance Cove, from where the iron ore was shipped.

After the mines closed, many residents moved from Bell Island. About 2,500 people live there in 2024. As you ride around Bell Island, you encounter stunning views of the bay

and attractions including a lighthouse, the mine tour, a series of murals, Dick's Fish & Chips, and more.

When you're ready, return to Portugal Cove and take Route 21 for 13 kilometres north to Bauline. This fishing community (population 412) with its winding roads and steep hills is situated on the shores of Conception Bay.

From Bauline, head northeast along Pouch Cove Line for 7 kilometres to reach Pouch Cove (population 2,063), which faces the Atlantic Ocean. Pouch Cove has some of the longest slipways (boat ramp or launch) in the province.

At Pouch Cove, take Route 20, ride south for 8 kilometres, and turn left into Flatrock (population 1,722). Its parish church has a grotto resembling that in Lourdes, France. Flatrock is another prime place to stop for a stroll and scan the water for whales.

Continue on Route 20 to Torbay (population 7,852), named for a similar looking town in Devon, England. Turn onto Marine Drive for a coastal route through the town of Logy Bay-Middle Cove-Outer Cove. At the end of Marine Drive, turn left onto Route 30 and continue to Water Street in downtown St. John's.

Ride along Water Street and turn left on Blackhead Road to Route 11 and back to Petty Harbour-Maddox Cove.

HOWLEY
BADGER
GAMBO
STEPHENVILLE
GOOBIES
PORT AUX
BASQUES
ST. JOHN'S

45 **Channel-Port aux Basques to Stephenville**

Distance: 332 km

46 **Stephenville to Howley**

Distance: 344 km

47 **Howley to Badger**

Distance: 332 km

48 **Badger to Gambo**

Distance: 340 km

49 **Gambo to Goobies**

Distance: 276 km

50 **Goobies to St. John's**

Distance: 324 km

Index of Place Names

Abraham's Cove, 34, 37
Aguathuna, 33
Allan's Island, 222
Anchor Point, 83
Appleton, 152
Aquaforte, 242
Arches Provincial Park, 66
Argentia, 229
Arnold's Cove, 226
Avalon Peninsula, 225-57
Avondale, 250

Bacon Cove, 250
Badger, 121
Badger's Quay, 177
Baie Verte (town), 101, 103
Baie Verte Peninsula, 101-9
Baine Harbour, 215-26
Bareneed, 248
Barr'd Islands, 168
Bartlett's Harbour, 71
Bauline, 257
Bay Bulls, 241-44
Bay de Verde Peninsula, 235-39
Bay L'Argent, 138, 211, 213
Bay of Islands, 45-50
Bay Roberts, 248
Bay St. George, 29-31
Baytona, 150
Beachside, 111
Beaumont, 117
Beaumont North, 117
Bellburns, 67
Belleoram, 139-40
Bellevue, 227
Bellevue Beach, 227
Bell Island, 256
Benton, 187
Birchy Bay, 150
Birchy Head, 54
Bird Cove, 75

Bishop's Falls, 121, 124
Black Duck Cove, 159
Black Duck Pond, 248
Blackhead, 253
Blanc-Sablon (Quebec), 77
Blow Me Down, 248
Boat Harbour, 216
Bonavista (town), 206
Bonavista Peninsula, 199-206
Boswarlos, 34
Bottle Cove, 49
Botwood, 127
Boutte du Cap Park, 35
Boxey, 140
Boyd's Cove, 155
Branch, 233
Brent's Cove, 107, 109
Bridgeport, 157
Brig Bay, 73, 75
Brighton, 118
Brigus, 248
Britannia, 193-95
Broad Cove, 239
Brookfield, 177
Brookside, 216
Brown's Arm, 143, 145
Brownsdale, 236
Buchans, 121
Bull Arm, 225
Bulls Cove, 219-20
Bunyan's Cove, 191
Burgeo, 39-42
Burgoyne's Cove, 195-96
Burin (town), 219-20
Burin Bay Arm, 219-21
Burin Peninsula, 209-22
Burlington, 107-8
Burnside, 182-84
Burnt Islands, 18

Calmer, 222
Campbell's Creek, 34
Campbellton, 149
Cape Anguille, 23, 26, 29
Cape Broyle, 241-42
Cape Ray, 23, 24

Cape St. George, 29, 34-35
Cape St. Mary's Ecological Reserve, 233
Cappahayden, 242
Capstan Island, 80
Carmanville, 173-74
Cat's Cove, 250
Cavendish, 235
Centreville, 179
Chamberlains, 250
Champney's West, 200
Chance Cove, 226-27
Change Islands, 163-65
Channel-Port aux Basques, 17-20, 23, 26
Chapel Arm, 227
Chapel Cove, 250
Charlottetown, 188
Clarenville, 193, 197
Clifton, 195
Clode Sound, 191
Coachman's Cove, 101, 103
Cobbler Island, 118
Cobb's Arm, 158
Codroy Valley, 23-26
Colinet, 233
Collins Cove, 219
Come by Chance, 225
Comfort Cove-Newstead, 150
Conception Bay South (CBS), 250
Conception Harbour, 248
Conche, 93, 95
Connaigre Peninsula, 133-41
Conne River, 133-35
Coomb's Cove, 137, 139-40
Corner Brook, 49-50
Cottel Island, 182-84
Cottlesville, 157
Cottrell's Cove, 130
Cow Head, 59, 62
Cox's Cove, 50
Crabbes River Park, 29-31

Croque, 93
Crow Head, 160
Culls Harbour, 181
Cupids, 247-48

Daniel's Harbour, 66-67
Davidsville, 174
Deadman's Bay, 176
Deep Bay, 168
Deer Lake, 52, 57, 97
De Grau, 34
Dildo, 235
Doyles, 23
Dunfield, 199
Dunville, 229
Durrell, 160

Eastport, 181-85
Eddies Cove (East), 83
Eddies Cove West, 71, 83
Elliston, 200
Embree, 145
Englee, 93, 95
English Harbour, 200
English Harbour East, 211
English Harbour West, 140
Epwikek, 31

Farewell, 163, 167
Ferryland, 242
Fischells, 29-30
Flat Bay, 31
Flat Bay West, 31
Flatrock, 257
Fleur de Lys, 101, 104
Flowers Cove, 83
Fogo (town), 170-71
Fogo Island, 167-71
Forteau, 78
Fortune Harbour, 130
Fox Cove, 220
Fox Roost, 17
Foxtrap, 250
Francois, 41-42
Frenchman's Cove Provincial Park, 222
Freshwater, 229

Gambo, 179, 187
Gander, 151-52, 173-79
Gander Bay, 150
Garnish, 219, 222
Gaultois, 41, 135
Gillams, 50
Gillard's Cove, 160
Glenburnie, 54
Glenwood, 152
Glovers Harbour, 129
Glovertown, 181, 187
Goobies, 209-10, 225
Goose Cove, 199
Gooseberry Cove, 231-33
Grand Bank, 222
Grand Falls-Windsor, 121-24
Grandois-St. Juliens, 93
Grates Cove, 237
Great Harbour Deep, 98
Great Northern Peninsula, 52, 65-99
Green Cove, 158
Green's Harbour, 235
Greenspond, 179
Grey River, 41-42
Gros Morne National Park, 52-62

Hamilton Sound, 174
Hampden, 99
Hant's Harbour, 236
Happy Adventure, 185
Harbour Breton, 137
Harbour Grace, 247
Harbour LeCou, 17-20
Harbour Main, 250
Harbour Mille, 209, 213
Harbour Round, 107, 109
Hare Bay, 179
Harris Point, 173
Harry's Harbour, 113
Hawke's Bay, 67
Hayward's Cove, 181
Heart's Content, 236
Heart's Delight-Islington, 236
Heart's Desire, 236

Heatherton, 29
Hermitage, 41, 133-35
Herring Neck, 158
Hibb's Hole, 248
Hickman's Harbour, 193
High Beach, 222
Highlands, 29-30
Hillgrade, 157
Holyrood, 250
Horwood, 150
Howley, 97-98
Hughes Brook, 49
Humber River Valley, 49
Hussey's Cove, 248

Indian Bay, 179
Irishtown-Summerside, 49
Island Harbour, 168
Isle aux Morts, 18

Jackson's Arm, 97-98
Jackson's Cove, 113
Jamestown, 197
Jeffrey's, 30
Joe Batt's Arm, 168
Journois, 31
J.T. Cheeseman Park, 23
Keels, 205
Kelligrews, 250
Kettle Cove, 160
King's Cove, 204-5
King's Point, 113
Kingston, 239
Kitchuses, 250
Knights's Cove, 205

L'Anse-Amour, 78
L'Anse-au-Clair, 77, 78
L'Anse-au-Loup,78, 80
L'Anse aux Meadows National Historic Site, 52, 83-87
Labrador, 77-81
Lady Cove, 193
Lamaline, 222
Lance Cove, 256
La Poile, 20
Lark Harbour, 49

LaScie, 107, 109
Laurenceton, 145
Lawn, 222
Lawrence Pond, 250
Leading Tickles, 130
Lethbridge, 187, 191, 196
Lewisporte, 143, 149-52
Little Bay Islands, 117
Little Burnt Bay, 145-47
Little Harbour, 159
Little Harbour East, 213
Little Rapids, 50
Little St. Lawrence, 221
Logy Bay-Middle Cove-Outer Cove, 257
Long Harbour-Mount Arlington Heights, 227
Long Island, 116
Long Pond, 250
Lourdes, 37
Lower Cove, 34
Lower Lance Cove, 193, 195
Low Point, 239
Lumsden, 176
Lushes Bight, 116-17

Main Brook, 90, 93, 95
Main Point, 173-74
Manuels, 250
Manuel's Cove, 160
Marble Mountain, 49, 97
Margaree, 17
Martin's Point, 61
Marystown, 209, 215, 219
McCallum, 41, 135
McIvers, 50
Meadows, 50
Merritt's Harbour, 158
Middle Arm, 108
Midland, 97
Miles Cove, 115
Millertown, 121
Millville, 26
Milton, 193
Ming's Bight, 107-8
Mint Brook, 179

Monroe, 195
Moore's Cove, 130
Moreton's Harbour, 157
Mortier, 220
Mount Carmel, 233, 244
Mount Pearl, 247, 250
Musgrave Harbour, 174, 176
Musgravetown, 191

New Burnt Cove, 195
New Chelsea, 236
New Ferolle, 73
New Harbour, 239
New Melbourne, 236
New Perlican, 236
Newstead, 150
Newtown, 176
New World Island, 155-60
Nickey's Nose Cove, 113
Norman's Cove-Long Cove, 227
Norris Arm, 143
Norris Point, 55, 59-60
Northern Arm, 128, 130
North Harbour, 210

Old Perlican, 236-37
Open Hall, 203
Otterbury, 248

Pacquet, 107-8
Parkers Cove, 216
Parson's Pond, 65
Pasadena, 97, 99
Patrick's Cove-Angels Cove, 233
Peterview, 127
Petite Forte, 216
Petley, 193-95
Petty Harbour-Maddox Cove, 253
Phillips Head, 130
Piccadilly, 37
Pick Eyes, 248
Pidgeon Cove-St. Barbe, 77
Pike's Arm, 158
Pilley's Island, 116

Pinware River Provincial Park, 81
Placentia, 229, 331
Plate Cove East, 203
Plate Cove West, 203
Plum Point, 71, 73, 77, 89-91
Point Leamington, 128
Point May, 222
Point of Bay, 130
Pollards Point, 98
Pool's Cove, 138-39
Pool's Island, 177
Port Albert, 163
Port Anson, 115
Port au Bras, 220
Port au Choix, 68-69
Port au Port Peninsula, 29, 33-37
Port au Port West, 33
Port aux Basques, 17-20, 23
Port Blandford, 189
Port de Grave (town), 248
Port de Grave Peninsula, 248
Porterville, 145
Port Rexton, 199-200
Port Saunders, 68
Port Union, 200
Portland, 197
Portugal Cove South, 242
Portugal Cove-St. Phillips, 254-57
Pouch Cove, 257
Purcell's Harbour, 159

Quirpon, 85

Ramea, 41
Random Island, 193-97
Red Bay, 77, 81
Red Cliff, 203
Red Harbour, 215
Red Head Cove, 237
Reef's Harbour, 73
Reef's Harbour-Shoal Cove West-New Ferolle, 71, 73

Reidville, 52

Rencontre East, 137-38, 211

Renews, 242

Riverhead, 244

River of Ponds, 67

Robert's Arm, 115

Robinson's, 30

Rock Harbour, 215

Rocky Harbour, 59-61

Roddickton-Bide Arm, 95

Rodgers Cove, 151

Roger's Cove, 158

Rose Blanche, 17-20

Rushoon, 215

Sally's Cove, 61

Salmon Cove, 239

Salvage, 185

Sandbanks Provincial Park, 39

Sandy Cove, 185

Savage Cove, 83

Seal Cove (Baie Verte Peninsula), 101

Seal Cove (Conception Bay), 250

Seldom Come By, 167

Shalloway Cove, 181

Sheppardville, 101, 107

Ship Cove (Burin Peninsula), 231

Ship Cove (Connaigre Peninsula), 219

Ship Cove (Port de Grave Peninsula), 248

Ship Cove-Lower Cove-Jerry's Nose (Port au Port Peninsula), 34

Shoal Bay, 168

Shoal Brook, 54

Shoal Harbour, 193

Shoe Cove, 107, 109

Sibley's Cove, 236

Silver Spring, 250

Sop's Arm, 98

South Brook, 97, 115-18

South Dildo, 235

South East Bight, 216

Southern Arm, 111

Southern Bay, 199

Spaniard's Bay, 248

Spanish Room, 215

Springdale, 111-13

St. Alban's, 33-35

St. Andrew's, 24-25

St. Anthony, 83, 85, 89-90

St. Anthony Bight, 89

St. Bernard's-Jacques Fontaine, 211

St. Brendan's, 181-82

St. Bride's, 233

St. Catherine's, 244

St. Chad's, 182

Steady Brook, 49

Stephenville, 33

St. Fintan's, 29-30

St. Jacques, 139

St. John's, 247, 250, 254

St. Joseph's Cove-St. Veronica's, 133

St. Lawrence, 221

St. Lunaire-Griquet, 85

St. Mary's, 244

Stoneville, 163

St. Patricks, 111

St. Paul's, 62

St. Pierre and Miquelon, 209, 222

St. Teresa, 31

St. Vincent's, 241, 243-44

Summerford, 157

Summerville, 203

Sunnyside, 225

Sweet Bay, 203

Swift Current, 210

Tablelands, 55-57

Table Point Ecological Reserve, 67

Terra Nova (town), 188

Terra Nova National Park, 181, 187-91

Terrenceville, 211

Three Mile Rock, 65, 69

Three Rock Cove, 35, 37

Tickle Cove, 203-4

Tilting, 167-70

Tilton, 239

Tizzard's Harbour, 157

Tompkins, 24

Toogood Arm, 158

Topsail, 250

Torbay, 257

Tors Cove, 241

Traytown, 181

Trepassey, 243

Trinity, 179, 199

Trinity Bight, 200

Trout River, 52, 57

Trouty, 199

Turk's Cove, 236

Turtle Creek, 150

Twillingate, 155-60

Upper Amherst Cove, 205

Upper Gullies, 250

Valleyfield, 177

Valley Pond, 157

Virgin Arm-Carter's Cove, 157

Wareham, 179

Waterville, 95

Wesleyville, 177

Western Brook Pond, 62

Westport, 101, 104

West St. Modeste, 80

Whitbourne, 229

Whiteway, 235

Wild Cove, 101, 103

Wiltondale, 52, 54, 59

Winter Brook, 193, 197

Winterton, 236

Witless Bay, 241

Woodstock, 107-8

Woody Point, 54-57

Wreck Cove, 140

Wreckhouse, 23

Note from the Author

Photography and motorcycling constitute a large part of my good weather days in Newfoundland and Labrador. I've travelled to all corners of the province, especially the island portion (the Rock). My buddies and I have travelled by motorcycles all over eastern Canada and the US. But most of my motorcycling has been in this Canadian province.

The motorcycle is reason enough to go each day, as I do love riding. In the spring and fall, electrically heated jacket and gloves help extend the riding season. A decade or more ago, I decided to get back into SLR photography and then started to document the province as I travelled it. Conversations with the people I meet are also a big part of each day.

—Harry O'Reilly